PRACTICAL WEEKEND PROJECTS

for Woodworkers

35 Projects to Make for Every Room of Your Home

PHILLIP GARDENER AND
ANDY STANDING

Fox Chapel
PUBLISHING

This book is a collection of previously published material. Portions of this book have been reproduced from *The Weekend Woodworker* (978-1-55870-533-3, 1999) and *Weekend Routing Projects* (978-1-84537-776-2, 2006).

ISBN 978-1-5048-0106-5

Library of Congress Cataloging-in-Publication Data

Names: Gardner, Phillip, author. | Standing, Andy, author.
Title: Practical weekend projects for woodworkers / Phillip Gardner, Andy Standing.
Description: Mount Joy : Fox Chapel Publishing, 2018. | Includes index.
Identifiers: LCCN 2018028290 | ISBN 9781504801065
Subjects: LCSH: House furnishings. | Woodwork.
Classification: LCC TT194 .G37 2018 | DDC 684/.08--dc23
LC record available at https://lccn.loc.gov/2018028290

We are always looking for talented authors. To submit an idea, please send a brief inquiry to acquisitions@foxchapelpublishing.com.

Printed in China
Fourth Printing

Project and studio photography: Edward Allwright

Step-by-step photography for Bookends, Mug Shelf, Table Lamp, Tray, Shoe Rack, Knife Block, Jewelry Box, Wastepaper Basket, Mirror, Side Table, Traditional Cupboard, and Paneled Coffee Table: Andy Standing

Illustrations for Kid's Bed, Adirondack Chair, Shelf Unit, Bathroom Accessories, Console Table, Birdhouse, Single Wardrobe, Privacy Screen, "Waney" Shelves, Kitchen Accessories, Stackable Storage Units, Corner Cupboard, Picture Rail Shelf, Modernist Coffee Table, Mailbox, Vanity, Tall Storage Chest, Kitchen Sink Makeover, and Modernist Cupboard projects: Paul Griffin

Contents

Working Safely

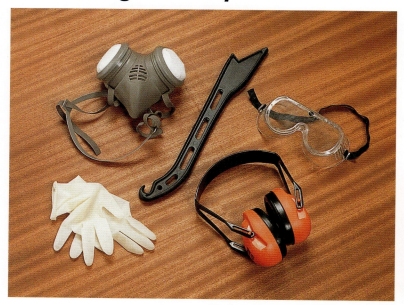

A basic health and safety kit (clockwise from bottom left): surgical gloves, respirator, push stick (for pushing wood through a circular saw or table-mounted router), goggles, and earmuffs.

At all times be sure to follow any recommendations provided by tool manufacturers or rental shops regarding health and safety—garnished with some common sense, of course. Remember, we're not going to be in your workshop to shout, "Don't do that!"

Dust Extraction

Sawdust is a serious hazard for woodworkers. The image of the gray-haired craftsman toiling away in his workshop, up to his knees in shavings and sawdust, might evoke a romantic nostalgia, but the reality is rather different. Not only does sawdust make a terrible mess of your workshop, it can also affect your health. Inhaling the dust produced by hardwoods and man-made boards such as MDF will cause irritation and can lead to serious illness. Try to remove as much dust as possible at the source, by connecting your power tool to a dedicated workshop vacuum cleaner. These machines are specifically designed to cope with fine dust and also often incorporate features such as automatic switching, which means that the vacuum operation can be controlled with the power switch on the tool.

Introduction

This book is intended for both the novice "weekend carpenter" and those who have some basic skills and want to improve the scope and quality of their work. Hopefully, the newcomer will discover an insight into how to design and construct individual pieces of furniture for the home and garden—everything suggested as a project is both cost-effective and reasonably simple to achieve, using an absolute minimum of complicated joints or techniques—while more experienced readers will pick up ideas about contemporary design, which they can then adapt to more advanced working methods, should they wish.

While all the projects can be constructed exactly as the designs shown using the suggested methods and techniques, though not all the items will be to everybody's requirements, and adaptations from the basics are always possible. It will be a fairly straightforward task to adjust the dimensions of the plans to suit your particular needs, but try to keep the proportions the same. Scale drawings or cardboard models can help to modify the designs, the easiest scale to work to being 1:10. Note that the measuring conventions used throughout the book are always length first, followed by width, and then thickness. Feel free to experiment with different kinds of wood, too, but remember to buy the best quality that you can afford, as it will greatly improve the finished piece.

On the following pages, you will find general information about materials and the tools you'll need, as well as basic techniques—these will be invaluable to the newcomer, and a useful reference to the more experienced hobbyist. There follows more than 35 projects to make, from simple shelves and kitchenware to an ambitious chest of drawers.

For anyone who enjoys carpentry as a hobby, this book will hopefully come as a breath of fresh air, with pages and pages of contemporary and stylish furniture that you will love to have in your home, and that can be made in one weekend, or across several.

Difficulty Ratings

 Ideal beginner's project

 Perfect for those who have some experience with woodworking

 Ambitious projects that experienced carpenters will enjoy making

Tools, Equipment, Wood, and Hardware

Any hobby is going to entail the purchase of some equipment. You will have more success with woodworking if you work with wood that has been accurately cut to size and planed to a consistent thickness. To do this efficiently, you need the right tools.

The basic toolkit—a set of screwdrivers, hammer, electric drill, etc.— does not need to be explained in detail. Nevertheless, this chapter discusses the more specialized tools needed to complete some of the projects in this book.

Don't fall into the common trap of finding tools so attractive that you buy ones for which you have no real need. Instead, build up a kit slowly, always buying the best quality and brand that you can afford.

Where to buy your tools also needs consideration. Flea markets and garage sales are good hunting grounds for bargain-priced secondhand tools, but rarely for new tools, since these tend to be low-quality imports or knockoffs. You need to have a reasonable knowledge of tools before buying in such places because there are no guarantees and defects may not be immediately apparent.

Large DIY stores have a wide range of reasonably priced tools, but for specialized, quality equipment you will need to visit a dedicated tool store, usually staffed by helpful, knowledgeable people. Many of the larger stores offer excellent online ordering. Buy tools from well-known manufacturers with a reputation for quality, since they will want to maintain that reputation.

Hand Tools

These are rarely employed in professional workshops since the demands of productivity preclude their use. But for the cost-conscious weekend carpenter who may not have a lot of space, they are a sensible starting point.

Measuring and Marking

Marking and measuring tools should always be of the best quality. You will need a measuring tape and steel ruler for general measuring, and a sliding T-bevel for marking angles as well as a utility knife, marking gauge, and square. Always check the accuracy of a square; I have seen cheap versions of my 4 in. (100 mm) square with a blade inaccuracy of $\frac{1}{32}$ in. (1 mm) over the short length of the blade. If you use a tool such as this, your work will never be true, and you will waste your time and materials.

As you grow in your woodworking abilities, further options would be a mortise gauge, a marking gauge, and some basic drafting tools such as a combination square, an adjustable set square, and a pair of compasses and dividers. Another extremely useful tool is the digital caliper, which will give you accurate measurements of wood thickness, rabbet depths, and so on. Finally, you will need an endless supply of sharp pencils.

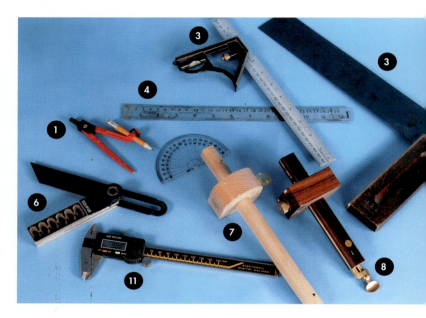

Marking and measuring 1 pair of compasses, 2 dividers, 3 squares, 4 ruler, 5 knife, 6 sliding bevel, 7 marking gauge, 8 mortise gauge, 9 straightedge, 10 adjustable square, 11 digital caliper, 12 vernier gauge

Saws

A good basic collection of saws would consist of a crosscut or general-purpose saw, for cutting across the grain of wood (don't buy the disposable "hard point" type because these saws are mainly for site work and cannot be sharpened), backsaw a.k.a. tenon saw (the better models of these have a brass back), coping saw for cutting curves, and a hacksaw for cutting metal.

Good additions to your kit would be a frame miter saw for angled cuts and, for fine work, a dovetail saw (a smaller version of a backsaw). Buy a miter saw that can cut compound miters—the additional expense is well worth it: one will pay for itself in terms of time saved and frustration avoided.

You might also want to try a pull saw. This, as its name suggests, cuts on the pull stroke. It is easy to use and leaves a fine finish.

Saws 1 crosscut saw, 2 backsaw, 3 hacksaw, 4 coping saw, 5 miter saw, 6 pull saw

Chisels, Gouges, and Screwdrivers

You will need a small set of chisels for squaring mortises and other purposes. They can be bought in sets and there are two types: bevel-edge and firmers. The more versatile bevel-edge chisel is a light tool that gives increased control and accuracy; the side bevels allow one to cut into tight corners.

Firmers are the chisels you hit with a mallet. The blade is far stronger and can be used in a robust manner. If you buy the "split-proof" variety, they can take repeated mallet blows with no damage.

Other additions to the toolkit include a gouge (for paring), which is just a chisel with a curved end, a mortise chisel (an extremely strong firmer chisel for removing the waste from a deep mortise), a wide range of screwdrivers, and an awl.

Chisels and screwdrivers 1 firmer chisels, 2 bevel edge chisels, 3 flathead screwdrivers, 4 awl, 5 Phillips screwdrivers, 6 gouge, 7 mortise chisel, 8 Yankee screwdriver

Hand Planes and Scrapers

A plane is needed to smooth the rough surface left by the saw, and also to prepare boards for jointing. Planes are maybe the most difficult hand tools for the novice to master. A common misconception about planes is that you can buy one, sharpen it, and then achieve the silky-smooth finish of the cabinetmaker in moments. You can't. The plane is a precision tool made of finely calculated components, but to achieve the accuracy and ease of use you require, it will need even further refining. When a plane is made, the casting will be machined flat, but it is never truly flat. The blade also will have imperfections and will need polishing. These defects should be corrected and adjusted before any plane is used.

There are several basic types of plane. The jack plane, available in two widths,

Planes and scrapers: 1 jack plane, 2 flat cabinet scraper, 3 shoulder plane, 4 smoothing plane, 5 gooseneck cabinet scraper, 6 spokeshave, 7 block plane

is used for achieving a flat, level surface quickly. The smoother, or smoothing plane, is a shorter version of a jack plane and is good for general use; buy one of these when you start working in hardwoods. The block plane is a small and incredibly useful item; the angle of the blade is shallower than other planes and this tool is essential for planing end grain.

The shoulder plane is good for cleaning up the shoulders of tenons. A spokeshave—used for shaping surfaces—is a tricky tool to use, and is unnecessary if you are planning to buy an electric belt sander.

Two cabinet scrapers are shown in the photograph below—flat and gooseneck. These are superb woodworking tools, essential for hardwoods, but they are quite difficult for the novice to sharpen, until suddenly one day, almost as if by magic, you get the hang of it.

Sharpening Stones, Clamps, and Hammers

Of course, all these tools will need to be sharpened and maintained. You will need at least one good-quality sharpening stone, preferably an industrial diamond type.

A range of clamps will also be required—bar clamps for panels, speed clamps, webbing clamps for frames, and F- and G- clamps for all kinds of jobs—as well as a carpenter's vise or a workbench of some description. A portable workbench is a good compromise for the latter, at least in the early days.

You'll also want a medium-weight hammer and a pin hammer to cover your hammering needs. Use a mallet for driving chisels or persuading reluctant joints.

Clamps: 1 bar clamp, 2 speed clamp, 3 webbing clamp, 4 F- and G-clamps

medium-weight hammer

pin hammer

mallet

Power Tools

Power tools, whether outlet-powered or cordless, do take a lot of the hard work out of woodwork. Most power tools can be rented by the week or the weekend. It is usually better to rent from a small, independent company because the big chains more frequently service large construction companies that tend to rent for long periods, and short-term rental often works out to be more expensive.

Power Drill and Bits

A power drill is a necessity; virtually every carpenter owns at least one. These can be either powered straight from the outlet or by battery. The latter is more expensive but much easier to use since you are not restricted to trailing lengths of cable. The minimum power required is 12 volts with a quick (one-hour) charge.

For each job, you will need a selection of drill bits. These are designed for masonry, metal, or wood and graduate in ⅟₃₂ in. (1 mm) increments. High-speed-steel bits, normally called HSS bits, are general-purpose bits, used for both wood and metal.

"Spur" or wood bits have a flatter cutting profile with a small point or spur in the center. This locates the center of the drill and stops the bit from "wandering."

Flat bits offer a crude but effective method for the drilling of larger-diameter holes when accuracy is not imperative.

A hole cutter is pricey, but accurate and long-lasting; it will cut both wood and metal.

The multispeed bit is also quite expensive and is only really necessary if you envisage doing a lot of work with the same size drill, such as fitting cylinder locks.

Also of use are plug cutters, employed in the making of the Adirondack Chair on page 206 and the Duckboard on page 89. A slightly better type with four cutters is also available, with the advantage of being self-centering.

Jigsaw

A jigsaw is an essential tool that can cope with many different jobs and materials due to the wide range of available blades. Buy one that has an electronic

Drill bits: the red case holds HSS twist drill bits, the gray case contains "spur" or wood bits. The remaining pieces include 1 multispeed bit, 2 hole cutter, 3 flat bits, 4 countersink bit, 5 masonry drill bit, 6 plug cutters.

The fine teeth of scrolling blades enable the jigsaw to be used for cutting elaborate curves. This model is fitted with a dust extractor adapter.

Jigsaw and circular saw

variable speed, giving greater control for curved cutting, and an adjustable pendulum cut—useful for ripping down the grain or coarse cutting of plywood. Another feature to look for is a method of clearing sawdust from the cut line, usually by blowing the dust away. Blades can be bought in mixed packs, but it's best to just the types you need for a particular job, fine-toothed scrolling blades being a top choice. Carbon-steel blades are the best by far. The black plastic plate is a shield that fits over the metal shoe of the saw, preventing any scratching on lumber. The small clear plastic part is an anti-split device: because the jigsaw cuts on the up stroke, it can tear delicate lumbers or plywood when cutting across the grain; this plate, inserted around the blade, minimizes that effect.

Circular Saw, Planer, and Power Sander

A circular saw and electric planer are good additions to the collection, but they are not an immediate necessity. A circular saw is ideal for dealing with long, straight cuts. A range of blades is available for the circular saw: crosscut, ripping, or combination. There is also a fine-finish blade, giving a quality of cut that just needs the barest planing subsequently. Always buy blades with tungsten tips.

Blades for a circular saw (left) are available in diameters from about 5 $^{15}/_{16}$–10 in. (150–256 mm). An electric plane is useful, but not essential for the newcomer.

Sanding machines will make the tedious aspects of carpentry—smoothing and polishing your projects—more bearable. There are three basic types: the belt sander, the palm or orbital sander, and a small triangular tool called a detail sander. If you are only going to buy one, choose a random orbital model because it is the most versatile. Orbital sanders come in a range of sizes and finishing capabilities; essentially, the smaller the circular motion of the

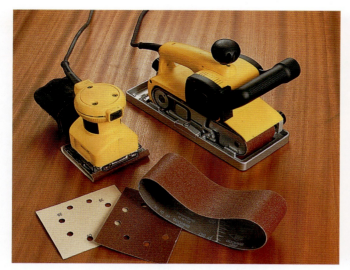

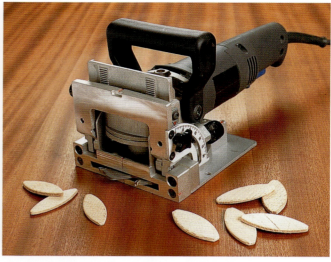

An orbital sander (left) and a belt sander (right). Sanding sheets for both types appear below.

The strong edge-to-edge joints that can be achieved by using a biscuit jointer make the tool ideal for joining boards to make tabletops.

sanding plate, the finer the finish. The belt sander above is fitted with a sanding frame, which allows regular removal of waste on a flat surface without "dishing." It is an excellent attachment, but it doesn't replace a plane! A detail sander (not shown) is useful for awkward access work.

Biscuit Jointer and Grinder

Another time-saving device is a biscuit jointer. This is a small circular saw with a thicker than normal blade that cuts a groove to a predetermined depth. Small oval "biscuits" are then glued in the groove, bridging two adjoining pieces of lumber and providing a strong joint, either edge-to-edge, at right angles, or at any division of a right angle.

An electric grinding wheel, while not an essential item, will prove a boon when putting a hollow-ground edge on planes and chisels. Combined with a quality grinding jig, it will take any guesswork out of achieving razor-sharp tools.

Finally, there's the router.

Planer

Random orbital sander

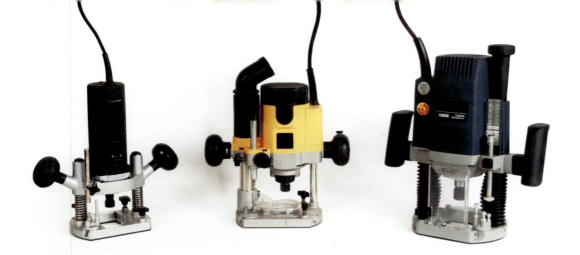

The Router

The router has—in recent years—been wholeheartedly embraced by the weekend woodworker. It is a sort of cross between a drill and a jigsaw, but on the other hand, like neither. It is actually a handheld version of a machine from the joiner's shop called a **spindle molder**, with a chuck, like a drill, called a **collet**. **Cutters** are placed in the collet like a drill bit, the main difference being that once the cutter has entered the surface of the wood, you can move the tool and cutter in any direction. This enables you to cut channels through the middle of the wood or intricate moldings on the edges with superb accuracy.

While the router is often used as purely a means to machine decorative parts and edges, by far the most useful aspect for the weekend woodworker is its ability to cut precise joints every time, thereby overcoming a major skill barrier and allowing entry for all into the craft of woodworking. The array of cutters available will give you the capability to cut housings, rabbets, mortise and tenons, and dovetails—in fact, any of the simple joints used in this book.

Even though these tools have only recently started to have a huge impact on the hobbyist market, they have been in existence since the early 1900s. Consequently, the range of accessories and cutters is vast, with constant additions to both. This enables

Routers are produced in a range of different sizes. The smallest, shown on the left, is easy to handle and economical to buy, though only powerful enough to cope with light jobs. The mid-sized model in the center is a versatile machine with a more powerful motor and sophisticated features, suitable for more sustained use. The machine on the right is a heavyweight tool with a ½ in. (12 mm) collet. It can cope with most jobs and is powerful enough to drive the largest cutters.

This router is a medium-size model with a fully adjustable fence. Also shown is a small range of cutters and guide bushes (to be used in conjunction with plywood templates).

the weekend woodworker to have access to the sophisticated machining possibilities of the joiner's shop, resulting in great savings of time and money. However, they can appear to be mysterious and intimidating machines. This chapter will help you to understand how the tool works and learn how to use it safely and effectively.

Anatomy of a Router

Dust-extraction nozzle. Can be an integral part of the base or a separate accessory. It is a vital part, and should always be used in conjunction with a powerful workshop vacuum.

Variable speed control. This allows you to adjust the speed to suit the cutter. The larger the cutter, the slower the speed you need. Speeds range from around 8,000 to 24,000 rpm.

Motor. Router motors for lightweight tasks can be as small as 500 watts; for heavy professional use, and to drive the largest cutters, motors in excess of 2,000 watts are used.

Depth adjuster. This feature controls the exact depth to which the router is plunged. It must be accurate and easy to set.

Plunge lock. This grips the supporting pillars and holds the main body in position when the cutter is plunged into the workpiece.

Power switch. Often incorporated into one of the handles. Some may be locked in the "on" position; others must be gripped to keep the machine operating.

Handles. Usually mounted on both sides of the motor. They must be comfortable and easy to hold, giving you firm control over the machine. Sometimes incorporate plunge lock and/or switch.

Adjustable side fence. Attaches to the base with a pair of rods and is used to guide the machine along a straight edge.

Collet and nut. The equivalent of a chuck on a drill. It holds the cutter and must be machined to a high tolerance because the cutters spin very fast, and any play would lead to vibration and poor performance. Collets range in size from ¼–½ in. (6–12 mm).

Depth-setting turret. This sits beneath the depth adjuster and usually has three or more positions.

Guidebush. This screws to the bottom of the machine and is used with templates or jigs.

Collectable Cutters

Once you start doing a lot of routing, you will find that you begin to amass a collection of cutters, which come in a huge range of sizes and designs to suit differing jobs and materials. It is usually a false economy to buy a set of cutters because they often contain designs that you will never use. Buy good cutters, but since they are expensive, buy them only as you need them.

The majority of cutters on the market are TCT—tipped with tungsten carbide—because they are extremely durable and can be used on a wide range of materials. They can also be sharpened in the workshop using a diamond hone. Cutters are also commonly made from high-speed steel (HSS), which are cheaper than TCT cutters and capable of taking a much sharper edge. However, they are more easily blunted than TCT cutters and cannot be used on abrasive lumber or man-made boards.

Cutter Types

Straight. These are parallel-sided cutters, usually with cutting edges both on the sides and the base. They are available in a variety of sizes, from a diameter of less than 1/16 in. (2 mm) to around 2 in. (50 mm). Straight cutters are used for a range of jobs, from jointing to inlaying, and are the most versatile type of cutter.

Jointing. These specialty tools are the most complex types of cutter, and can be used for producing cabinet doors and various other joints simply and easily. They are normally suitable for use only in a router table.

Edge-forming. These are used to mold and shape the edges of a workpiece, usually for decoration. They are often self-guiding.

Trimming. These are straight cutters with guide bearings that can be used to follow templates or trim laminates and veneers.

Trial and Error and First Cuts

If you are new to routing, practice with the various cutters you buy on a piece of scrap wood before using them in earnest, partly to get used to the feel, but also to see just what each type of cutter can do. When making a cut, use two or three passes. If the wood smokes or the tone of the router drops, you are trying to remove too much material in one pass; stop, raise the cutter a little, and try again. Always allow the router to achieve full speed before starting a cut, and never start a cut with the cutter up against the wood.

It is important to familiarize yourself with the way the router works. The cutter rotates in a clockwise direction when viewed from above.

This means that if you plunge the cutter into a workpiece and push the router away from you, it will pull to the left. The "direction of feed" should always be against the direction in which the cutter rotates. Therefore, when pushing the router, the side fence must be mounted on the right. The tip of the cutter should pull the lumber along; if you rout in the other direction, there is a danger of the lumber being pushed away from the cutter, resulting in an uneven cut and the potential of danger to yourself from the exposed cutter.

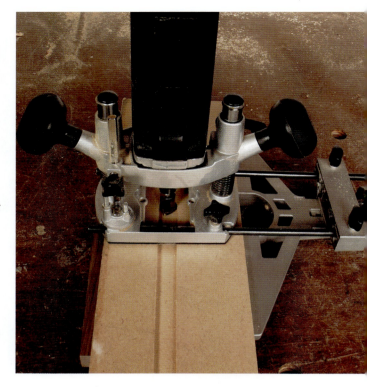

For your first attempt at routing, choose a simple task such as cutting a straight groove in a piece of softwood. Follow the steps below and take your time—before long you will be routing with confidence.

1 Clamp the workpiece firmly to the workbench, with its edge just overhanging the front. Draw a short pencil line parallel to the short edge and about 4 in. (100 mm) in.

2 With the power disconnected, stand the router upside down on the workbench and insert a straight cutter, ¼ in. (6 mm) in diameter. Make sure that at least three-quarters of the cutter shank is in the collet. Tighten securely with a spanner.

3 With the router upright, loosely fit the side fence to the right-hand side.

4 Stand the disconnected router on the workpiece and plunge the bit so that it just touches the surface. Engage the plunge lock. Place the bit on the marked line and adjust the fence so that it is tight against the edge.

5 To set the cutting depth, leave the cutter touching the surface and wind the depth-adjusting rod down so that it touches the turret. If possible, zero the scale and then wind the rod back the desired amount, which in this case is ³⁄₁₆ in. (4 mm). Lock the rod in place and release the plunge lock so that the router returns to the top of its travel.

6 You are now ready to make the cut. Before you do so, set the variable speed control to maximum (because you are using a small-diameter cutter), and check that all the adjustment screws are tight on the fence and depth adjuster. Connect the power and dust extractor.

◀ Position the router at the beginning of the cut. Make sure that the fence is tight against the side of the workpiece. Grip the handles and start the motor. When it is up to full speed, plunge the cutter into the workpiece and engage the plunge lock. Push the router forward, making sure that the side fence is still against the edge. It will now cut a straight groove.

Removing a Cutter

To release the cutter the collet must be pulled out of the central shaft by the collet nut. This means that the collet nut effectively has to be loosened twice. Initial loosening releases the pressure on the lower shoulder of the collet, and the nut may be turned by hand. The collet remains held in the shaft, so the cutter cannot be removed. As the nut is loosened, it begins to get stiff again as it contacts the upper shoulder of the collet. A spanner is now needed: this time the nut will pull the collet from the tapered shaft, and it will then release its grip on the bit.

Get the Speed Right

Make sure that you move the tool at the optimum speed. If you move too slowly, the bit will overheat and there will be burn marks on the workpiece; too fast and the motor will strain and the cutting process will be difficult. With practice, you will soon get a feel for it. When you reach the end of the cut, release the plunge lock and let the cutter rise out of the workpiece. Turn off the motor and, once it has stopped, put the router aside.

Rules of Routing

Routing may look a little complicated, but that isn't the case as long as you follow these simple rules:

- Protect yourself—use a dust extractor and wear safety glasses, earmuffs, and a dust mask.

- Make sure the workpiece is securely clamped to the bench before you start. Position any clamps so that they will not interfere with the router's movement.

- Look after the cutters and keep them sharp. Always unplug the router before changing cutters.

- Never tighten the collet nut without a cutter fitted. This can cause serious damage to the collet, and may even break it, so always leave the nut loose.

- Plan your work carefully. Have a "dry run," with the router switched off, to ensure that no problems arise.

- Use the variable speed function to suit the cutter and feed rate. Large cutters need slower speeds. Always set the cutter to the appropriate full speed before beginning your cut.

- Check all settings, and make sure that everything is tightened before starting work.

- Make several shallow cuts rather than one deep one. Never make a cut deeper than the diameter of the cutter you are using in one pass. For example, to make a groove 5/16 in. (8 mm) deep, make two passes each 1/8 in. (3 mm) deep, followed by a 1/16 in. (2 mm) pass. This puts less strain on the machine.

Guiding the Router

Aside from the type of cutter used, the router's versatility stems from one other main factor: the method used to guide the machine. In detailed woodworking, the router must be steered precisely into the workpiece to produce accurate results. There are several methods of achieving this.

Side fence

Most routers have a removable side fence; the novice woodworker should always use it, since it's the easiest way to guide the router. However, this will only work on straight edges, and its use is limited by the length of the mounting rods. Adding a second fence is a great help when cutting mortises on the edge of lumber, because it will stop the router from rocking from side to side.

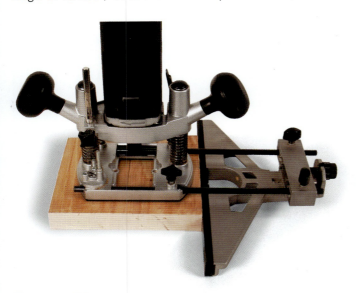

Trammel bar

To cut circles or arcs, a trammel bar or circle-cutting jig can be used. These are ideal for shaping circular tabletops.

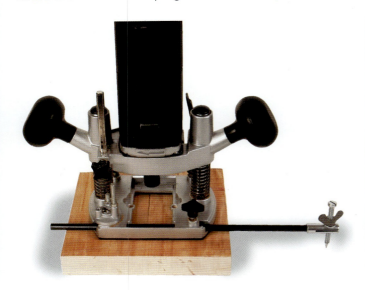

Guidebush

Another very common method is to use a template in conjunction with a guidebush. A selection of bushes is provided with better makes of router. Guidebushes are screwed to the underside of the router, with the cutter protruding through the bush. The outer edge of the guide bush is then held against the template, usually shaped from a small piece of plywood or MDF, allowing repeated shapes to be cut with accuracy.

Bearing-guided cutters

These cutters are self-guiding and will run along the edge of a shaped workpiece without needing a fence or any additional guide. They produce consistent results. When using one, you must go around it in a counterclockwise direction. However, when molding an internal edge such as a frame, go in a clockwise direction. This means that you are feeding the work against the direction of bit rotation, making the machine bite into the lumber and push back against the operator. If you try to reverse these directions, the machine will be pulling away from you all the time. This makes the router dangerous and difficult to control, particularly if using large-diameter cutters.

Freehand

Some woodworkers can, after considerable practice, use a router freehand for operations such as carving letters or decorative features, much in the same way a jigsaw can be used. This is something that will help develop your control of the router. Use a V-groove cutter on a piece of scrap wood and make a shallow cut. Observe how the cutter tries to pull the router off-line and how the grain pattern affects this.

Guide batten

For cutting housings and grooves in the center of boards, a guide batten (or a pair of battens) clamped to the surface may be used. The router baseplate can be run along the side of the batten or sandwiched between a pair of battens, so there is no chance of it wandering off-line.

Router Table

Once equipped with a router and some good quality cutters, you might wish to invest in a **router table**—it is probably the most useful accessory that you can get for your router. In fact there are situations where the router needs to be mounted in a specially made router table. The router is mounted under the table with the cutter protruding above the table, allowing the lumber to be manually pushed past the cutter. This will allow you to use the larger jointing and molding cutters, provided that you have a powerful enough router, and also to undertake operations that are either difficult or dangerous to attempt using a handheld router.

Look for router table of sturdy construction with a comprehensive instruction manual. A good router table must have a flat and supportive surface, the

The direction of the feed is important

larger the better, and a sturdy fence. A sliding miter fence is also useful, especially for molding end grain.

Setting the depth of cut can be a problem, because, since the router is inverted, the power of the return springs and gravity both work against you. A fine height adjuster can be fitted to your router to ease these difficulties. For safety reasons, a separate power switch should be attached to the front of the table in a convenient position so that the router can be easily controlled. The machine's own power switch should be permanently fixed in the "on" position when table-mounted.

Like routers, there are many designs of router table on the market. The main requirements are that the table and fence should be strong and sturdy.

Wood and Hardware

Lumber and Boards

Essentially there are two types of lumber: **softwood** and **hardwood**. Hardwood is by far the more expensive, but for some furniture it is the only realistic material. Softwood includes the various species of pine and is sold in a vast array of stock sizes and qualities. It is sold as either "sawn"—unfinished and rough—or S4S ("surfaced," or planed, on all four sides). The size quoted is always of the rough lumber before it was planed. When the lumber has been planed on all four faces to achieve the S4S state, the section has been reduced by about ³⁄₁₆ in. (5 mm) in both directions; 2 x 2 in. (50 x 50 mm) S4S is, in fact, about 1¾ x 1¾ in. (45 x 45 mm). Only buy sawn lumber if you want to feature the rough finish, as with the Corner Cupboard on page 200.

For simple tasks, such as the Kid's Bed on page 54 you can buy S4S lumber from an ordinary building supply store or a DIY store. However, always remember that the stock size will have lost that few millimeters!

In the main, buy your lumber from a good local building supply store or lumberyard. These should have a policy of allowing you to select your own lumber, and you'll soon develop a good relationship with the sales staff. If you tell them what you need the wood for (furniture), they will help you select the best lengths and quality. Look for defects such as splits, cupping (warping across the width), winding, large knots, and small black dead knots, and politely reject any lumber of this sort.

The sources above are also the places to buy beading, moldings, dowel rods, and boards or sheet material. Many places will cut boards to size, although they may insist that you buy the entire sheet when cut.

Prior to starting work, lumber should be left in the workshop or home for a week or so, to acclimatize to the ambient temperature. Always stack your wood flat and support it well.

For hardwoods and paper-backed or iron-on veneers, you will need to visit a more specialized store; these are usually advertised in woodworking magazines. A visit to your local cabinetmaker will prove useful, since they often sell on small quantities of excess lumber at reasonable rates. The same criteria regarding defects and storage apply as to softwoods.

Of the boards used in this book, MDF (medium-density fiberboard) is a smooth, highly stable board that finishes very well. Always check that the corners haven't been damaged or that steel packing bands have not destroyed the edges, and reject any board that is offered with these defects. Shuttering plywood is probably the cheapest form of board available, used in the construction industry for boarding up and making molds for pouring concrete. Only use this board when the surface will be completely covered, as in the Kitchen Sink Makeover on page 180.

Birch-faced plywood is a reasonably priced board with a surface that will rarely require more than a light sanding in preparation.

You can, of course, use reclaimed materials. Purchase them from a respectable seller, or better still, keep your eyes open for building sites where places are being renovated—restaurant and bar refurbishments tend to be the most rewarding hunting grounds. Just ask the site foreman what is being sold off: hardwood doors, counters, and strip flooring are firm favorites. You will have to arrange transportation and storage and then undertake the onerous task of de-nailing, which is extremely tedious, but you'll save a fortune.

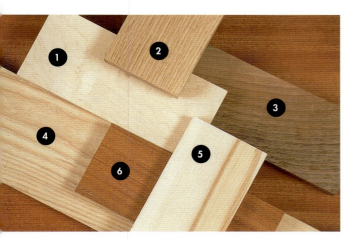

Hardwoods: 1 burr maple, 2 ash, 3 walnut, 4 American oak, 5 maple, 6 mahogany

Hardwood and softwood moldings and pine, shown here in both sawn and S4S states

Hardware

As a catchall heading, hardware is a bit of a misnomer, since many fittings are often made of plastic or brass. However, this category does include all the traditional items associated with connecting lumber, i.e., screws, nails, and nuts and bolts.

The large DIY stores tend to have the widest range of fasteners and fittings, and most stock the products you will require for simple furniture making: magnetic catches, mirror plates, small dowel rods, and door supplies. Just about everything is sold in small packs, and you might have to buy in multiples when you only need one or two items. These packs can also work out to be quite expensive when compared to buying one or two of the same piece from a small hardware store.

There are some items that you will only find in a hardware store. Usually, however, these stores are not open on the weekend and the waiting time during the week can be lengthy. A good solution is to inquire if they provide online ordering or a mail-order service—most do.

A good source for many items is a marine supply store, aka boat chandler's. These will supply most fittings, such as hinges, in good-quality brass or stainless steel. The stainless steel rod used in the Waney Shelves on page 192 can be bought from a supplier and cut to length with a hacksaw.

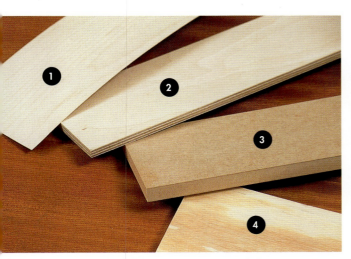

Sheet materials: 1 Paper-backed veneer, 2 birch-faced plywood, 3 MDF, and 4 shuttering plywood are the sheet materials used in this book.

Hardware: Corner blocks, dowels, stretcher plates, mirror plates, magnetic catches, and other such fixings can be purchased inexpensively at DIY stores.

It's a good idea to buy a box of 100 or 200 screws for a job and put the surplus in a large plastic compartmentalized box. This means always having some on hand.

Don't be tempted to make do with fasteners and fixings that obviously weren't designed for the purpose—match the materials to the job.

The more specialized fittings, such as drawer runners and Blum hinges, can be purchased online.

Modern glues for woodworking: follow the manufacturer's directions for use at all times.

Adhesives

The vast array of wood adhesives on the market can be simplified for the weekend woodworker. First, a big favorite—two-part epoxy—is a remarkably strong glue. It is mainly used in boatbuilding and is widely available from marine supply or surf shops. Unfortunately, it is quite expensive.

You need to measure out the two components precisely and be aware of the ambient temperature. Use either plastic syringes or clear plastic containers marked on the side with graduations. The wearing of surgical gloves is advisable when mixing and applying epoxy, simply to protect your hands because the glue is difficult to remove from skin. When you use epoxy for the first few times, refer to the free data sheets provided.

PVA (polyvinyl acetate), the everyday white liquid glue that comes in plastic tubes, can also be purchased in a water-resistant version. Easy to use and cheap, it is not terribly strong, but adequate for most interior work.

Two-part filler, the elastic type, is often used in conjunction with lumber as a combination filler and adhesive. Buy it from a car paint supplier, where it should be considerably cheaper than a DIY store.

Filler adhesive needs to be applied with a caulk gun (mastic gun) and is sold under a variety of brand names. It is expensive, and once the tube is opened it goes off quite quickly, but it is ideal for rapidly gluing lumber that is not under any great stress.

Cascamite, a white, powdered resin glue mixed with water, is waterproof, dries clear, and is cheap and easy to use. Wear gloves when applying. It may have a different brand name locally.

Basic Woodworking Techniques

As you start working with wood, you will learn from the inevitable mistakes far better than any amount of book learning. There isn't a carpenter, or even for that matter a cabinetmaker, in the land who hasn't learned by the same process.

Marking Out

When your lumber is ready to work, you need to sort it into the best lengths for the job, taking into account the position of any knots; you don't want a knot where, at a later date, you will want to cut a mortise or other joint. Also, study the grain pattern, especially in hardwoods, and select it to the best advantage for the design.

The best tip ever: "**Measure twice, cut once**." Keep checking a measurement until you are absolutely sure before cutting. Remember, measuring and marking are the two main areas where woodworking mistakes occur. Once you have spoiled a couple of pieces of expensive lumber, you will appreciate the old saying!

Mark the proscribed length, leaving a small excess at each end, then square around from the marks using a **pencil** and a **try square** or **combination square**. Mark the line around all faces of the lumber to make it easier to keep your saw cut straight. If the marks don't line up perfectly, this means the wood is warped or "in wind" (where the lumber has started to spiral along its length), and this will have to be rectified. Choose the best face and edge and then mark accordingly.

Normally a **sharp pencil** is fine, except where accuracy is essential. In these cases use a **utility knife**, but a professional cabinetmaker will always use a dedicated **marking knife**. This has a cutting edge on one side only, allowing the knife to rest precisely against the tape measure or square.

Measuring the piece of lumber

Marking off the first face

Continuing the line onto the next face

Marking gauge: used to mark a thickness

Mortise gauge: a marking device with twin spurs

A **marking gauge** is used to cut or score a line parallel to the edge of a piece of lumber. Hold the stock firmly against the edge of the lumber and roll the spur into the wood. Be aware of the direction of the grain and run the tool along the lumber in such a way that the grain pulls the point of the gauge away from the stock.

A **mortise gauge** is a similar tool; here, two parallel lines are scored simultaneously, defining the waste portions of a tenon and the mortise. By using the same setting to mark both parts of the joint, in theory a perfect fit is always obtained.

To mark an oblique line, use a **sliding T-bevel**, which has an adjustable blade that allows you to set and repeat any angle at will.

A **rod (story pole)** is a simple measuring stick and is described in more detail on page 30. This is used when making up mortise-and-tenoned frames, as in the Modernist Cupboard on page 172.

When marking shelves or anything that has a left and right pair, ensure that you mark each piece as such. It helps to lay out the components on the bench or floor and visualize how they fit together prior to marking out housings and rabbets, etc.

When marking several identical pieces, measure the first and then use it as a template for the others. This minimizes measuring errors, assuming that you have managed to cut the first piece to the right length. Professional cabinetmakers often use devices called setting-out rods, which are effectively large boards with all the dimensions of a project marked on them. The maker then only needs to lay the lumber on the board and mark off the relevant dimension.

Prepping Lumber by Hand

As long as you have selected it carefully, planed softwood will require minimum preparation—usually just light planing to remove small ridges that run across the grain as a result of the lumber being machined too quickly. If you buy hardwoods ready-machined, the same concept applies, but this is expensive. Preparing hardwood yourself takes diligence and is not easy.

For perfect preparation of hardwoods, cut the lumber slightly over length and secure it level in a vise. Use a jack plane to get the best face perfectly flat. The edge of the plane's sole can be used as a guide to assess low points, both across the grain and along it. Hold the plane tilted at 45 degrees on the lumber and look for any gaps under the plane. If you can see light anywhere, this means that you have a low spot and the rest of the wood will need to be planed down to that lowest level.

To check for straightness over the length, lay two flat and parallel **winding sticks** across the lumber at front and back; sight down the lumber from one end, making sure that the tops of both sticks are parallel to each other. If not, the lumber should be planed diagonally, taking off the high points.

Once you have achieved a flat surface, turn the lumber in the vise so that the best edge is uppermost. Plane the edge true and square to the first face. Use the plane to check for light showing through, but also use a square to ensure that the edge remains at 90 degrees to the planed face. Release from the vise and mark with face and edge marks.

Hold the stock of a **marking gauge** hard against the finished face and slide the bar back and forth until the spur is the required distance from the face. At no point should the lumber be thinner than this set distance. Lock the gauge and, holding the lumber against the bench, slightly roll the gauge so that the spur leaves a cut line in the edge. Do this on all four edges.

Replace the lumber in the vise and plane the other face down to the lines. When this face is flat and parallel to the other, set your marking gauge to the desired width, mark across both faces and ends with the stock tight against the face edge, and plane down to the marks once more. After you have done all this, you should have a flat, true, and square piece of lumber.

Using a Story Pole

All the marks are placed on the rod, which is then laid against all the components and the marks from the rod are transferred across all together, saving time and eliminating any possibility of error.

The most important marks are those between the shoulders of any joints; excess lengths of tenons or the horns of a door stile can be removed later. Note the use of ticks instead of straight lines: this improves accuracy, especially when marking out boards.

To mark out a board, use the largest square you possess and a straightedge. Always start from the best corner and ensure that the tape or ruler runs parallel to the edge of the board.

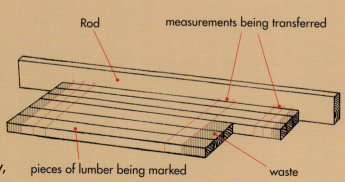

Rod

measurements being transferred

pieces of lumber being marked

waste

Planing

After sawing, the surface of the lumber will need to be planed. When planing, keep the shavings fine by setting the adjusting nut to take fine shavings, and be aware of the direction of the grain—plane with the grain at all times. In most lumbers you can see the grain direction by looking at the edges: if the grain on the edge runs up to the left-hand side of the face, you will have to plane from right to left, and the reverse is obviously true. This method is not infallible, because sometimes in the middle of a piece you will find what is known as "wild grain." In some lumbers, such as mahogany, this can be seen as a slightly darker area, and a very light brush with your fingertips will confirm it. (If you run your finger along the surface of the lumber, you can usually feel which direction is the smoother, though be careful not to get a splinter . . .)

Wild grain can be combated in two ways: try planing with the plane at 45 degrees to the direction of travel, or rub a small amount of beeswax across the sole.

The **block plane** is held in the palm of one hand and used to plane end grain and to put an "arris" on lumber. An arris is a small bevel used as a detail or, on painted furniture, to prevent the paint from being knocked off the corners.

For rapid and effortless planning, use an **electric plane**; the same principles apply as for a hand plane, with the addition that you must be careful when starting and finishing a pass. If the body dips at all when coming to the edge of the lumber, an ugly gouge will result.

Never use an electric plane closer than about $1/64$ in. (0.5 mm) to the finished line, and always finish with a jack plane, which gives you greater control and a far superior finish.

All electric planes have a fine depth adjuster, but I tend to use my left-hand forefinger and thumb for superfine adjustment of the cut depth with a slight upward pressure. I also adjust the level of the sole with this hand when planing a bevel. Always keep your hands well away from the blades and check that the blade rest (if fitted) is in position before setting the tool down.

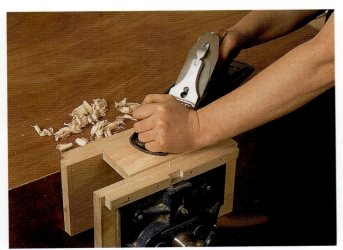
Skew the plan at 45 degrees to combat wild grain

Using a block plane to create an arris

Cabinet Scraping

As mentioned earlier, cabinet scraping is an essential technique to master when finishing hardwoods. Although at first glance a cabinet scraper looks just like a square of plain steel, all four edges have a very slight angle ground on them that leaves a burr. After burnishing the burr, a sharp cutting edge is achieved.

Hold the tool in both hands at about 45 degrees to the lumber and slightly flex it. As you push (or pull) the tool along the work, very fine shavings will be removed. If you remove dust as opposed to shavings, your scraper needs sharpening (see page 35). Don't run the scraper absolutely in line with the grain, always at a slight angle, varying the direction with each stroke, but never scrape at right angles to the grain.

The finish left by a well-sharpened scraper is incomparable; the tool is also used to disguise tears in the surface of the lumber. To do this you will have to gradually dish the surface to the depth of the tear.

The main problem with using a cabinet scraper is that it becomes warm with friction quickly, and you must take care not to burn your thumbs.

Finishing hardwood with a cabinet scraper

Chiseling

Work that needs to be chiseled will usually be done in one of two ways. First, cutting—or more correctly, **paring**—in a horizontal plane. A typical example for this would be smoothing the cheeks of a sawn tenon.

For this type of paring, the work must always be mounted in the vise or securely clamped to the bench. Keep the tool level and grip the cutting end tightly, exerting a downward pressure with your thumb. Start each thin slice with a corner of the cutting edge and slide the tool across any high points. The back of the chisel must always lie flat against the surface—if you lift the handle while cutting, you will dig into the lumber.

Paring the cheeks of a tenon

Horizontal paring of the grain

The final cut will use the line made by the mortise gauge as a starting point, and the edge of the chisel will slot into the cut line at the front on the end grain. As you push forward toward the shoulder of the tenon, be aware of the gauge lines at each side; as these come into view from the top, it is time to stop. Finally, by pressing down hard with your thumb, assess any high points in the middle and remove them with a slicing action.

When removing waste from lumber that can be approached from both sides, such as a housing or dovetail socket, chisel to just past the middle of the cut then approach it from the other side. Repeat this technique until you have cut down to the gauge lines.

This will leave a small hump in the middle, which is removed at the end. To retain full control of the tool, take a small slice at a time.

The other technique is **vertical paring**; this is the same as horizontal paring, except that here the work is placed on the bench with the chisel held vertically and downward pressure removes the waste. Always protect the surface of the bench by using a small piece of cardboard or waste lumber. Generally speaking, vertical paring is used to remove waste in a speedy fashion, changing to horizontal paring when you approach the final line or when greater accuracy is required; however, personal preference will play a part as to which method finds favor with you.

Sawing

Before you start to cut any workpiece, always make sure that the work is well supported and level. And always cut along the waste side of the line. This means that the pencil line should still be visible on the piece of lumber after you have made the cut.

A handsaw is held with the forefinger extended along the handle to guide the direction of the blade in both planes. When starting a cut, use the thumb of the other hand as a guide, with the tip of your thumb just up to the line and the extreme tip resting against the saw blade. Hold the handle with a loose grip and make a few gentle strokes back and forth, using the lower half of the blade to start the cut. Western handsaws cut when they are pushed (Japanese

Crosscutting across the grain of the lumber

Ripping to reduce the width of a board

Crosscut vs. Rip

There are two basic saw cuts: crosscutting and ripping. Crosscutting means cutting across the grain of the lumber. A backsaw (tenon saw) is ideal for crosscutting smaller pieces; for larger pieces, use a crosscut saw or panel saw. Ripping is cutting along the grain, to reduce the width of a board. The ripsaw, crosscut saw, or panel saw may be used for this.

Alternatively, use a wooden bench hook to steady the workpiece. This is a simple piece of equipment that hooks over the edge of your workbench and stops the wood from slipping.

Miters are 45-degree cuts in two parts that are then joined together with a biscuit or pins to form a right angle. The most basic method is to use a backsaw (tenon saw) in a miter box, but this is rarely satisfactory because the saw can move from side to side—and when the box becomes worn with use, the error is compounded. A frame saw is a far better solution. Mark the cut with a combination square or a miter square, and hold the lumber firmly in the frame using a clamp. Take it slowly, and keep an eye on the line.

A compound miter is a miter with a bevel on two planes; this bevel is marked out and then planed with a sharp block plane.

Using a handsaw: note the extended forefinger that guides the direction of the blade

When cutting sheet material or ripping down a plank with an electric saw, use a guide clamped to the work. This is necessary for both circular saws and jigsaws, although with a circular saw ensure that the batten or clamps will not obstruct the passage of the saw's motor.

models, however, cut when pulled), so let the saw do the work on the downstroke, using a smooth sweeping action, and pull the saw back effortlessly. Gradually increase the length of the strokes.

Always check that the blade's face remains at 90 degrees to the face of the work, and control this by use of your extended forefinger. When coming to the end of a cut, ensure that the waste piece is held or supported in some way, so that it will not tear off.

When using a power saw, make sure that the lead is long enough to complete the cut and that it will not get snagged.

Jigsawing with a guide

Biscuit Jointing

Biscuits are tightly compressed ovals made from beech which, when wetted with glue, expand into a slot precut by the jointer and provide a strong method of joining lumber edge to edge. The biscuits come in three sizes: 0, 10, and 20, with size 0 being the smallest.

A benefit of the jointer is its built-in margin of error of about ¼ in. (6 mm). In addition, marking out is extremely simple, in most cases being just a small mark on the face of each lumber to be joined.

You can use the biscuit jointer as a freehand tool with the work clamped down, or you can attach it to the bench with small blocks or screw through the sole plate (if holes are provided). In the latter case, the material to be slotted is then pushed up to the cutter.

Using biscuits to join the parts of a tabletop

Sharpening Tools

There is not one project in this book that can be completed satisfactorily unless your tools are absolutely sharp.

For plane blades and chisels, a hollow-ground bevel should be put on the edge first. The term "hollow-ground" refers to the slightly dished profile that results from using a grinding wheel. It is possible to grind this primary bevel flat on a stone, but the ease with which you can put on a fine cutting edge later makes a huge difference to the finish and time taken. Set your jig to grind at 30 degrees and lay the plane blade or chisel against the jig as shown in the photograph below.

Slowly bring the tool into contact with the wheel, keeping it firmly pressed to the jig. When contact is made, slide the blade back and forth along the wheel, dipping the blade in water every couple of passes to keep it cool. This will avoid "bluing" the steel; if the steel does blue, you must grind off all traces of the discoloration and start again—this is a waste of expensive tool steel, so take great care. After some time there is a possibility that your wheel

Sharpening a plane iron in a jig

Dressing a wheel with a diamond dresser

Honing a chisel using a honing guide

Sharpening a cabinet scraper

will become pitted or grooved, in which case you will have to dress the wheel with a diamond dresser. Better-quality jigs will have an attachment that allows you to do this.

To put the honing edge on, use a honing guide on a diamond stone, as shown. Diamond stones may be an expensive option, but they do not dish like the more traditional stones, and consequently last far longer.

To achieve the sharper edge, the angle needs to be 25 degrees. Hold the chisel or plane blade as shown and move it back and forth, keeping the blade firmly pressed down on the stone.

When an even edge has been produced in this way, there will be a burr on the reverse of the tool, which must be removed by laying the back of the tool flat on the stone and rubbing back and forth. It is essential that the tool remains flat while doing this. When smooth, a fine burr is left on the extreme tip; this is removed by drawing the edge of the tool through some end grain, usually the end of a workbench.

All cabinet scrapers are manufactured sharp with the cutting burr ready to use; however, in use this will quickly dull and the tool will need to be re-sharpened. First, file the long edges square to the face, then put a bevel of about 80 degrees on using a stone; the photograph above shows a silicon

Cutters are kept sharp with a diamond stone and light oil

carbide stone for variety, but a diamond stone is preferable.

At the very least, sharpen both long edges—some woodworkers do all four, it's up to you. This grinding creates the burr that provides the cutting edge, so do not remove it as one would with a plane or chisel. Next, rub the back of the burred edge with a burnisher. This burnisher is a rounded steel tool, similar to that used by a butcher in days of old to sharpen his knives with great dramatic effect. You can use the back of a gouge for this job, although there are some devices on the market that claim to make this job easier.

Router cutters and electric saw blades can be sharpened using an ordinary diamond stone, but the small one featured in the photograph above is particularly useful. Also pictured are some small wire brushes, PTFE spray, and light oil. All these items can be kept together as a kit, with the express use of keeping your router cutters sharp and cutting at maximum efficiency.

Simple Joints

All of the joints used in this book are simple enough for even the novice to accomplish quickly.

There are two fundamental points to remember when producing an accurately fitting joint. First, always mark from a designated face. This is why we mark face side and face edge—not only do they provide reference marks as to which is the most attractive face, but they also ensure that the two component parts of a joint will be measured equally from the front of the item being jointed. Second, remove lumber as carefully as possible: to remove a little more is easy, to replace waste removed in error is not.

A **corner halving** is used to join two boards of equal thickness together. The amount of waste removed from both parts is the same and you will create a shoulder on both parts, which will keep the two boards at 90 degrees to each other. To determine the distance of the shoulders from the ends of both parts, proceed as follows:

Take one piece and lay it over the other, square to the lower piece at one end, making an "L" shape.

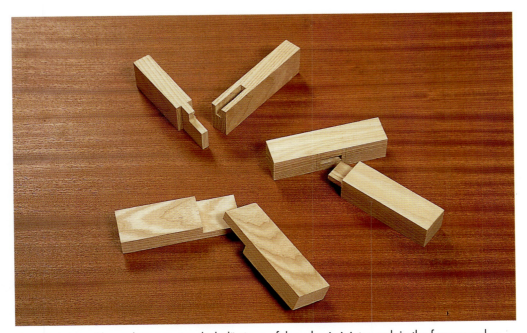

Simple joints. Shown here are "exploded" views of three basic joints used: in the foreground, a corner halving, used in the Corner Cupboard on page 200; on the right, a stub mortise and tenon, used in the Kid's Bed on page 54; and at the top, a haunched mortise and tenon, used in the Modernist Cupboard on page 172.

Draw a line on the lower piece where the upper one sits. Lay the two pieces side by side and copy the line across onto the other board. Square both lines around all four sides of each part.

Divide the thickness of the lumber in half and set a marking gauge to that dimension. Place the stock of the gauge against the face side and run a mark from the squared line on the edge up to the end grain, along the end grain, and then down the other side. Repeat for the mating part. Crosshatch the waste, this will be the upper portion on one piece and the lower on the other.

Place the board in the vise and saw down to the shoulder line with a backsaw as shown (below left). Turn the board around and cut from the other side. Then place the board vertically and cut the hump that will be left in the center, making sure you do not cut below the line at the rear.

Place horizontally in the vise and saw the shoulder line down to the gauge mark, ensuring that you keep an eye on the line at the rear of the work. Then clean up the saw cuts using a chisel.

This joint can be positioned not only at a corner but also in any place along the length of lumber, making a "T" or an "X" joint. In these cases, the waste has to be removed with a chisel after making two parallel saw cuts at the shoulder marks.

To make a **mortise and tenon joint**, mark the shoulders of the tenon as above but instead of dividing the thickness by two, divide by three. Saw the tenon cheeks as for the half lap, again finishing with a chisel.

For the mortise, use the gauge, again from the face side, to mark the full length of the mortise. Remove the waste down to the depth required, this being the same as the length of the tenon.

Use a drill bit with a diameter the same as the width of the mortise to remove the bulk of the waste. Then clean up the mortise hole with a chisel. For a far better finish, use a **router**. If you use a router the ends of the mortise will be rounded. Either square them off with a chisel or round off the corners of the tenon (the latter is usually quicker and easier).

If the tenon is a haunched or a **stub tenon**, place the board vertically in the vise and saw down the grain at the relevant points. If you are not sure about how the two parts fit together, it helps to cut the tenon and then place it in position prior to marking out the mortise.

Sawing to the shoulder line of a halving joint

Sawing a tenon cheek

Top: through housing joint; bottom: stopped housing joint

A **housing** is the term for a groove cut across the width of a board. Normally, this would be to slot a shelf into, as in the Shelf Unit on page 186. The two types shown are a "through housing" and a "stopped housing," the purpose of a stopped housing being to give a neater front edge to your work.

Mark two parallel lines the full width of the lumber that you are going to cut a housing into. These will be the shoulder lines and will be set apart the exact thickness of the shelf to be inserted.

Cut along the inside of the lines with a tenon saw down to the proscribed depth (usually halfway or a third into the thickness of the lumber). Use the straight cutting edge of the saw blade to assist getting the level cut all the way across the housing.

Remove the waste with a chisel, the first part with the cutting edge of the blade turned down. Approach from both ends working toward the middle, being careful not to cut into the shoulders in the early stages. A hump will be left in the middle of the channel; remove this by turning the chisel over and slicing the top until the entire channel is flat.

Hand-cutting a housing is arduous and time consuming, but a router or circular saw with the blade set to the correct depth will complete this task in moments.

If you are using a circular saw for a stopped housing, the final part will still need to be cut by hand using a chisel and a mallet.

Finishing

The final processes in the making of a project are also perhaps the most important. The first thing that people notice about any piece of woodwork is its finish. As the maker, you may be very proud of your neat jointing, or your rather innovative design, but unfortunately, unless the finish is perfect, these nuances will be ignored. Wood is a very tactile material so its feel is important.

Before any coating is applied, the surface must be free of imperfections. An experienced craftsman can produce a perfect surface by using just a plane; the rest of us, however, have to resort to abrasives.

Sanding

Modern sanding machines can make an excellent job of smoothing the roughest surface. Sandpaper is available in a variety of textures, from very coarse to very fine. A number followed by the word "grit" tells you how coarse it is; the lower the number, the coarser the paper. Work through several grades of sandpaper, starting with the coarsest and finishing with the smoothest—240-grit paper is usually fine enough to produce a surface that is good enough to accept a finish. Final sanding should be done by hand along the grain. If lumber is properly sanded it should begin to shine, because a smooth surface reflects light better than a rough one. All sharp edges should be "softened"—sanded until they are comfortable to touch. Sharp edges are prone to splintering and chipping, and so should be avoided.

Applying the Finish

Once the lumber has been prepared, choose a finish. Oil is versatile, easy to apply, durable, and can be repaired. The secret of achieving a good result is to build it up slowly. Start by applying a generous coat with a brush. Let this soak into the lumber for around 15 minutes. Then take a soft cloth and wipe away any excess. Wipe along the grain and pay particular attention to corners and recesses where the oil may collect. Now let the piece dry for at least 12 hours.

Once the surface is dry and hard, use 320-grit sandpaper to cut it back and remove any roughness, then apply another coat of oil, this time using a soft cloth and wiping along the grain, polishing the oil into the lumber. Again let the oil dry, though this should not take more than about four hours. Cut back with the sandpaper again and repeat the process. Continue doing this until the finish has built up to the desired level.

Projects for the Bedroom

42 Single Wardrobe

48 Mirror

54 Kid's Bed

60 Jewelry Box

66 Tall Storage Chest

72 Privacy Screen

Single Wardrobe

This simple project, designed to be constructed with the absolute minimum of tools and skills, is based on construction techniques used by scenic carpenters in theatre, television, and films. It uses triangular plywood plates and screws to replace the more usual jointing methods. This has two advantages: one, speed of construction, and the other, the materials can be easily recycled—so when you have tired of the wardrobe or your collection of designer suits has expanded beyond its capacity, you can unscrew it, remove the plywood plates, and adapt or expand it as required.

The seabird finials began as flaming Olympiad torches, but were adapted for ease of construction. You can, of course, indulge your own design talents, but remember that whatever shape you design as a finial will be constrained by the 2 x 2 in. (50 x 50 mm) section of the corner posts. The sides and door are constructed from thick tongue-and-groove boards, to avoid warping and to provide sufficient thickness for the hinge. The finish is a thin emulsion wash with a dash of PVA added. Poster paints with PVA are used for the finials.

Essential Tools & Materials

Tools
- pencil
- measuring tape
- combination square
- awl
- screwdriver
- hammer
- crosscut saw
- coping saw (or jigsaw with scrolling blade)
- power drill, $\frac{1}{8}$ in. (3 mm) wood bit, countersink bit
- workbench
- belt sander (optional)

Hardware etc.
- 100 countersink screws $1\frac{3}{16}$ in. (30 mm) x No. 6 gauge
- 2 magnetic catches
- $\frac{3}{4}$ in. (20 mm) panel pins
- handle
- 2 yard (2 meter) brass piano hinge, brass screws
- $\frac{3}{4}$ in. (20 mm) dowel rod or brass rail
- sandpaper in 80 and 100 grits
- PVA wood glue

Wood
- 12 pieces $78\frac{3}{4}$ x $4\frac{3}{8}$ x 1 in. (2000 x 112 x 25 mm) tongue-and-grooved pine or similar (usually sold as flooring-grade boards)
- 4 pieces $90\frac{9}{16}$ x 2 x 2 in. (2300 x 50 x 50 mm) pine or similar
- 256 x 2 x 1 in. (6500 x 50 x 25 mm) pine or similar
- 2 pieces 19 $\frac{11}{16}$ x 19 $\frac{11}{16}$ x $\frac{3}{8}$ in. (500 x 500 x 9 mm) plywood
- $17\frac{5}{16}$ x $77\frac{3}{16}$ x $\frac{1}{4}$ in. (440 x 1960 x 6 mm) plywood
- 16 pieces 4 x 4 x $5\frac{3}{4}$ in. (100 x 100 x 145 mm) triangular corner plates cut from $\frac{1}{4}$ in. (6 mm) plywood

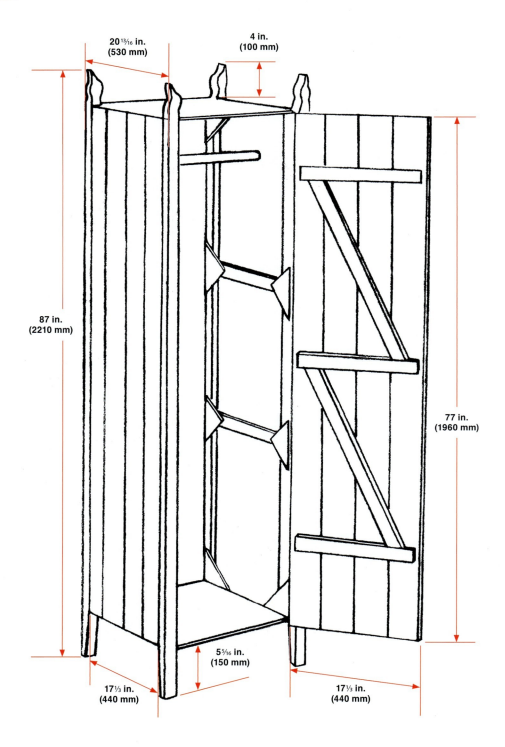

20¹³⁄₁₆ in.
(530 mm)

4 in.
(100 mm)

87 in.
(2210 mm)

77 in.
(1960 mm)

5⁵⁄₁₆ in.
(150 mm)

17⅓ in.
(440 mm)

17⅓ in.
(440 mm)

The sides and door are constructed from tongue-and-groove
boards ¾ in. (20 mm) thick. To cut costs, the side panels can just as
easily be constructed from ⅓ or ½ in. (9 or 12 mm) boards.

1

To construct the sides, begin by cutting eight lengths of tongue-and-groove to 77 in. (1960 mm). Select the best faces and position them in relation to each other, taking into account any warping or twist. Sort into two packs of four, slot together, and plane or saw off the tongue from the end board. Cut eight 2 x 1 in. (50 x 25 mm) battens to the full width of the panels. Place two equidistant from the center, and two ⅜ in. (9 mm) from the ends on each panel. Ensure that each batten lays square to the edges, and screw and glue them in place. Stagger the screws and use two per board; if you are using thinner boards—for instance, ¾, ½, or even ⅜ in. (19, 12 or 9 mm) thickness—you will need shorter screws. Make sure, however, that you use 1 in. (25 mm) boards for the door.

TIP

Brass or electro-plated piano hinges are often sold in 2 yard (2 meter) lengths. Cut to length with a hacksaw.

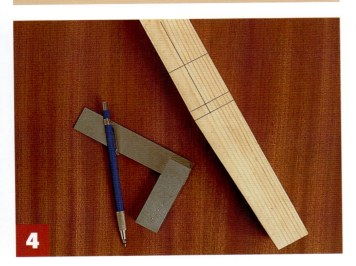

4

2 For the door, repeat step 1, except for the three battens, which will be 2 in. (50 mm) shorter. Place one batten in the center of the door, one 7⅞ in. (125 mm) from the top and one 11¹³⁄₁₆ in. (300 mm) from the base. The top of the door will be determined by which side will take the hinge—this has to be the edge from which you have removed the tongue. Ensure the battens lay square to the door edge, and are placed 1 in. (25 mm) in from the edges. Screw and glue in place as in step 1.

3

To determine the length and angle required for the diagonals, place a length in position, look down from above, and mark a line to cut to. Cut and screw and glue in place. Cut the four corner posts to 87 in. (2210 mm).

◀ Mark the best two faces on each post, then mark each post as "front left," "rear left," etc. From the base measure up 5¹⁵⁄₁₆ in. (150 mm), square round and mark a chamfer down to the base. The slope should run from the squared line taking ⁹⁄₁₆ in. (15 mm) off the two best (outer) faces at the base of each post. The picture above shows a corner post with the chamfers cut. It is also marked out to show the position of the ⅜ in. (9 mm) floor of the wardrobe, the position of a side strut for the side panel, and the amount of offset required when positioning the plywood plates to allow the door to close. This offset will be the thickness of the door, plus ¼ in. (6 mm) for the two front posts, but just ¼ in. (6 mm) for the two rear posts to allow a flush fit for the ¼ in. (6 mm) plywood back.

5

6

Mark out the position of the ⅜ in. (9 mm) plywood top on the corner posts, as shown by the two parallel lines. The distance from the upper mark to the bottom mark should be the height of the door, i.e. 77 in. (1960 mm). To achieve a consistent profile for the finials, cut a template from a scrap of ¼ in. (6 mm) plywood and draw your chosen design around it. Flip the template over for the left and right corner posts. Cut the profile with a coping or jigsaw, taking care to ensure that the cut is square to the front face and that the work is well supported.

When you have finished cutting all four finials, wrap some sandpaper around a tube of silicone or something similar and use it to smooth out the saw cut marks. If you have the use of a belt sander, the front end or "nose" of the tool is quite perfectly suited for this smoothing job.

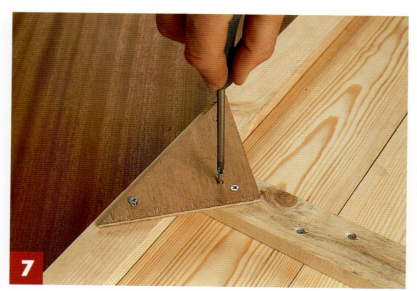

7

◄ To fit the side panels to the corner posts, select a pair of front and rear posts and arrange them parallel to each other with the outside faces down on the bench. Lay the side panel between the posts, ensuring that the panel is at the correct height in relation to the marks you made on the posts for the top and floor. At this point, the offset that you marked in step 3 becomes particularly important. Note the triangular plywood plate being screwed ¼ in. (6 mm) in from the edge of the rear post using No. 6 gauge countersink screws.

8

Use a waste piece of the correct thickness to help position the plate—the thickness of the door (¾ in. [20 mm]), plus ¼ in. (6 mm) in from the edge of the front post. Pre-drill the plates as shown and allow the screws to pull up the side panel so that it lies flush with the upper face of the corner post.

9

The dimensions of the top and floor might vary, but essentially the width will be that of the door plus the thickness of two battens, plus ¹⁄₁₆ in. (2 mm) for fitting the hinge. The depth will be the width of a side panel plus the thickness of two corner posts, minus the two offsets. Notice the plywood floor fitted to one side.

TIP

If you need to plane a bit from the door edge, remove the door, plane and then refit in place.

10

◄ Cut and true the plywood to size, then cut notches at each corner to accommodate the posts. To fit the top and floor, lay one side face down and screw the plywood in place. Rotate the entire assembly through 90 degrees onto the front face and fit the other side. To fit the back, put small waste piece blocks between the plywood plates at the back and set them in by ¼ in. (6 mm), the same as the rear plates. Check that the carcass is square, cut a ¼ in. (6 mm) plywood panel to fit, and attach with glue and pins. Rotate the carcass again so that the hinge side is face down. Fit the door, supporting the outer edge with a small block. Fit the hinge with screws every 15¾ in. (400 mm).

Mirror

Routers are particularly good at creating lengths of molding, and with a small selection of cutters, you can build up some impressive examples. This makes it easy to make your own frames for paintings, photographs, or mirrors. The molding on the frame of this swiveling dressing table mirror is made using a single cutter for both sides, and a pair of rabbets is cut on the inside to accommodate the mirror and the back panel. The design of the base has been kept plain, using the same cutter again for the edge molding.

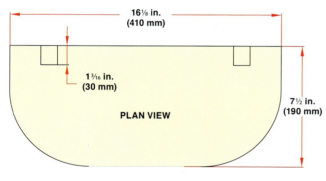

PLAN VIEW

16⅛ in. (410 mm)
1³⁄₁₆ in. (30 mm)
7½ in. (190 mm)

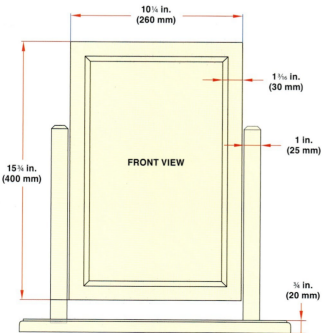

FRONT VIEW

10¼ in. (260 mm)
1³⁄₁₆ in. (30 mm)
1 in. (25 mm)
15¾ in. (400 mm)
¾ in. (20 mm)

Essential Tools & Materials

Tools

- measuring and marking tools
- coping saw (or jigsaw with scrolling blade)
- crosscut saw
- ripsaw
- miter saw
- band clamp
- power drill, plus bits: ¹⁄₁₆, ⅛, and ³⁄₁₆ in. (2, 3, 4, and 5 mm)
- screwdriver
- G-clamp
- Router, router table, bearing-guided rounding-over cutter, straight cutter: ½ in. (12 mm), bearing-guided chamfer cutter

Hardware etc.

- glue
- sandpaper
- mirror: ³⁄₁₆ in. (4 mm) thick, cut to size
- 10½ in. (12 mm) screws
- 200 2¾ in. (70 mm) screws
- washers

Wood

- 16⅛ x 7½ x ¾ in. (410 x 190 x 20 mm) English cherry (base)
- 2 pieces 11 ¹³⁄₁₆ x 1³⁄₁₆ x 1 in. (300 x 30 x 25 mm) English cherry (posts)
- 2 pieces 2¾ x ¾ x ⅜ in. (70 x 20 x 10 mm) English cherry (mounting blocks)
- 2 pieces 15¾ x 1³⁄₁₆ x ¾ in. (400 x 30 x 20 mm) American black walnut (frame sides)
- 2 pieces 10¼ x 1³⁄₁₆ x ¾ in. (260 x 30 x 20 mm) American black walnut (frame ends)
- 15 x 9⁷⁄₁₆ x ¼ in. (380 x 240 x 6 mm) plywood or MDF (back panel)

1

Cut the base to size with the crosscut and ripsaws. The ends need to be rounded. You can use templates or a compass, but the easiest way to do this is to find something circular that seems about the right diameter, such as a saucepan lid, place it over the corner, and draw around it. Cut around the corners with a jigsaw or a coping saw.

2

The top edge of the base is molded using a bearing-guided rounding-over cutter. Set the cutter sufficiently high in order for the vertical edge on the lower part of the cutter to cut into the surface. This gives a more defined edge, called a "quirk."

3

To make the frame, prepare the lumber to the size in the cutting list, but do not cut to length at this stage. You need to cut two rabbets on the inside face. First cut the one for the mirror itself using the straight cutter. This should be ⅜ in. (10mm) deep and about ³⁄₁₆ in. (5mm) wide. This assumes that your mirror is ³⁄₁₆ in. (4mm) thick and the back panel is ¼ in. (6mm) thick.

4

Cut a second rabbet. Move the fence back another ³⁄₁₆ in. (5 mm) or so and reduce the cutter height to cut a rabbet ¼ in. (6 mm) deep. Be careful doing this, since you are reducing the support underneath the workpiece. This makes it more liable to tip into the cutter, so guide the lumber carefully past the cutter.

5 Having completed the rabbets, replace the straight cutter with the bearing-guided rounding-over cutter, and using the same setting that you used on the base, mold the inside edge of the front of the frame.

6 Lower the cutter and mold the opposite side of the frame so it just rounds over the edge without forming a quirk.

7 Once the molding is complete, cut the frame components to length using the miter saw.

8 Glue and clamp the frame using a band clamp. Meanwhile, make the supporting posts for the mirror. Prepare to the dimensions in the cutting list but, as always, leave over-long. The sides of the posts are left square-edged but the tops are chamfered.

Molding End Grain

Molding end-grain can be fraught with difficulties, particularly on narrow components. Do not try to do it freehand, as it will end in disaster. The tip of the workpiece will catch on the cutter and you will not get a smooth cut. The simplest way to complete this cut is to clamp the post to a wider board. It is extremely important that this board has a perfectly square end. Hold both pieces hard against the fence and clamp up as shown in the picture. Alternatively, you can use a miter fence with a supporting board behind the workpiece.

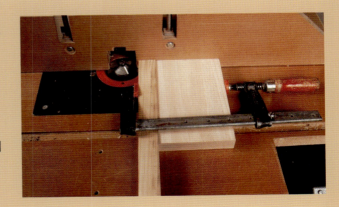

9 The bearing-guided chamfer cutter is used for this operation. Set the fence in line with the bearing, and the cutter high enough to take a reasonable chamfer. Start the router, run the workpiece slowly past it, and let the cutter run into the backing board.

10 Stop the router, remove the post, turn it over, and repeat the process until all four edges have been molded. The tops of the posts should look like this.

11 Take the assembled frame to your local glazier or glass shop so the mirror can be cut to fit.

12 Cut the back panel to size so that it fits in the rabbet. The back panel is screwed into place, so it is easy to replace the mirror. Drill holes ⅛ in. (3 mm) in diameter around the panel and countersink them. Put three across the bottom and top, and two on each side. The center of the sides will be covered by the mirror mounting blocks, so no attaching screw is needed. Screw the panel in place with the ½ in. (12 mm) screws.

13

◄ The mirror is suspended between the two posts on a pair of mounting blocks. You can miter the ends on the miter saw to improve their appearance, but since they will rarely be seen, this is not vital. Drill and countersink a pair of ⅛ in. (3mm) holes through the faces of them, and also bore and countersink a ³⁄₁₆ in. (4mm) hole through the side.

14 Screw the blocks in position on the rear of the mirror frame so that they are exactly on the centerline and flush with the outer edges of the frame.

15 Measure and mark the position of the mirror pivot points on the supporting posts. They should be 9 1/16 in. (230 mm) from the base, and in the center of the post. Drill a 1/16 in. (2 mm) pilot hole in both posts. Lay the mirror face down and screw through the mounting blocks into the posts. Place a thin washer on the screw between the mounting block and the post to provide a little clearance and to stop the mirror frame from hitting the posts.

16 Measure the position of the posts on the assembled frame and transfer this measurement to the base. Mark a center point on each position and drill a 3/16 in. (5 mm) hole through the base. Countersink on the underside.

17 Mark the center point on the base of each post and drill a 1/8 in. (3 mm) pilot hole. Be careful to keep the drill exactly in line with the post. Otherwise it will be difficult to position the post accurately.

18 ◄ Finally, lay the mirror on its back and screw through the base into the posts. Use 2 3/4 in. (70 mm) screws and put a dab of glue on the end of each post for added security.

Kid's Bed

This simple design uses low-cost materials, and a minimum skill level is required for the joints involved. The use of a router is recommended to cut the headboard housings. Although they can be cut by hand, it is a time-consuming business and a router will give you a far more professional finish.

The headboard and footboard could easily be adapted to your child's personal taste—for example, the headboard cut-out could be a silhouette of a favorite cartoon character; use a photocopier to enlarge a drawing and then paint the headboard to suit.

Before starting, take into account the size of mattress you will be using. I used one 6 ½ ft. (2 m) long by 31 $\frac{7}{16}$ in. (800 mm) wide, and all the measurements of the bed are designed to fit this size. If you use a different-size mattress, you will have to adapt the measurements.

I finished the bed by using a semi-matt paint on top of primer and undercoat, but you could use a color wash or stain, or just varnish. Gloss paint, however, could soon look tatty.

Essential Tools & Materials

Tools
- pencil
- straightedge
- measuring tape
- square
- marking gauge
- mortise gauge
- table-mounted circular saw (optional)
- router with ½ in. (12 mm) straight cutter
- screwdriver
- backsaw (tenon saw)
- jigsaw
- power drill, ½ in. (12 mm) flat bit, ⅛ in. (3 mm) twist bit, $\frac{5}{16}$ in. (8 mm) wood bit, ¼ in. (6 mm) multi-speed bit 7⅞ in. (125 mm) long
- ½ in. and 1 in. (12 and 25 mm) bevel-edge chisels
- mallet
- block plane
- workbench
- 2 sash clamps or 2 pairs of slow folding wedges

Hardware etc.
- 16 countersink screws 1 in. (25 mm) x No. 6
- 40 countersink screws $\frac{11}{16}$ in. (18 mm) x No. 6
- 8 "bunk-bed bolts" 4 in. (100 mm)
- PVA wood glue
- sandpaper in 80 to 150 grits

Wood
- 48 x 31⅞ x ½ in. (1220 x 810 x 12 mm) MDF
- 10 pieces 31$\frac{7}{16}$ x 4 x ½ in. (800 x 100 x 12 mm) plywood
- 2 pieces 35$\frac{7}{16}$ x 2 x 2 in. (900 x 50 x 50 mm) straight-grained pine or similar (S4S)
- 2 pieces 33$\frac{7}{16}$ x 2 x 2 in. (850 x 50 x 50 mm) straight-grained pine or similar (S4S)
- 2 pieces 82⅝ x 4 x 1 in. (2100 x 100 x 25 mm) straight-grained pine or similar (S4S)
- 2 pieces 78¾ x 1 x $\frac{9}{16}$ in. (2000 x 25 x 5 mm) softwood lipping

The dimensions of this bed make it suitable for a child of up to about 14 or 15 years old. As with many of the other projects in this book, you can adapt the dimensions and lists of materials to suit your own requirements.

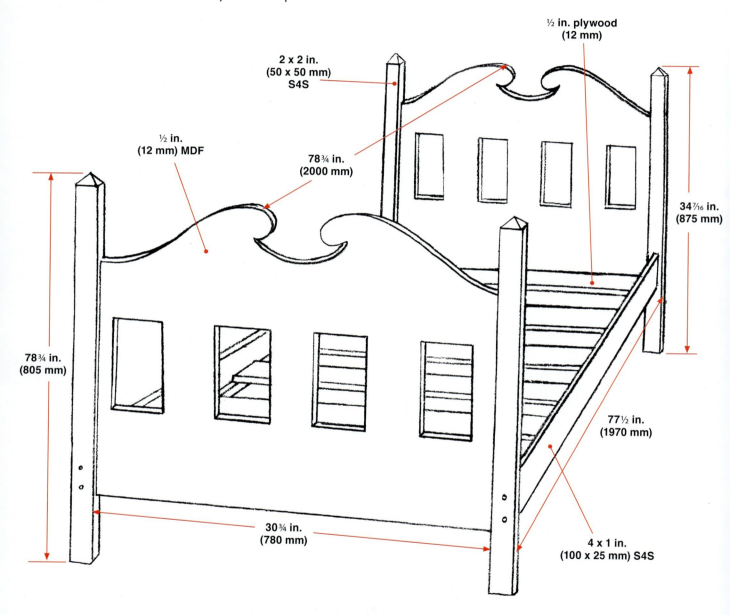

½ in. plywood
(12 mm)

2 x 2 in.
(50 x 50 mm)
S4S

½ in.
(12 mm) MDF

78¾ in.
(2000 mm)

34⁷⁄₁₆ in.
(875 mm)

78¾ in.
(805 mm)

77½ in.
(1970 mm)

30¾ in.
(780 mm)

4 x 1 in.
(100 x 25 mm) S4S

1

2

3

For the legs, you need two 35⁷⁄₁₆ in. (900 mm) and two 33⁷⁄₁₆ in. (850 mm) lengths of 2 x 2 in. (50 x 50 mm) lumber. Lay all four lengths side by side, with the best face uppermost and one end of all four legs aligned. Mark these faces as your face sides. Lay a square as near to the end of the four legs as you can and draw a line across all of them. This is the baseline of the legs, which will then need to be squared around each leg. Measure 8 in. (205 mm) from this line and draw another line across all four legs, to represent the bottom of the mortise for the side rails to enter. At this point you will need to measure accurately the true width of the 4 x 1 in. (100 x 25 mm) dimensioned lumber, normally about 3⁵⁄₈ in. (92 mm). Transfer this measurement to the legs so that the third line will be the width of the side rails along from the second line you drew. Transfer these two lines to the back of the legs. Set your mortise gauge to ½ in. (12 mm) between the pins, ⁹⁄₁₆ in. (15 mm) from the stock to the nearest pin. Then mark as shown.

TIP

Bunk-bed bolts might be difficult to locate, so track them down before you begin. You should be able to obtain them from a good hardware supplier, who will be able to order them if they are not in stock. Check online.

Separate the legs into two pairs and mark them left and right. On the inner face of each pair, mark out for the housings into which the headboard and footboard will fit. For the headboard, mark a line 20½ in. (520 mm) from the baseline, and for the footboard a line 17¾ in. (450 mm). Leave the pins of the mortise gauge set to ½ in. (12 mm), but adjust the stock to ⁹⁄₁₆ in. (15 mm), and mark as shown.

Clamp each leg to the bench, and use a router with a side fence to groove out the side channels to a depth of ⁹⁄₁₆ in. (15 mm). Turn each leg over and remove the mortise for the rails to a depth of ¹¹⁄₁₆ in. (18 mm). Mark the full height of each leg—for the head pair this is 34⁷⁄₁₆ in. (875 mm), and for the foot pair it is 31 ¹¹⁄₁₆ in. (805 mm). To finish the tops of the legs with a pyramid shape; measure 2 in. (50 mm) back from the top on each leg and make a 45-degree cut on all four sides. Cut the bottom of the legs to the line you first drew as the baseline in step 1.

From the 31 ⅞ in. (810 mm) edge of the MDF sheet measure 22 ¹³⁄₁₆ in. (580 mm) square across and cut the board into two pieces; the smaller one is the footboard. Working from the template on page 222, cut out the shape using a jigsaw fitted with a scrolling blade for the curves and a normal blade for the straight lines. Repeat for the headboard, but remember to extend the template so that the overall height is 25 ⁹⁄₁₆ in. (650 mm). Assemble each set of legs and board together and glue up, using sash clamps or slow folding wedges to hold the pieces in position.

Now take the two rails and cut them to a length of 80 ⅛ in. (2036 mm). Choose your face sides, turn them over and mark out for a stub tenon ¹¹⁄₁₆ in. (18 mm) long and ½ in. (12 mm) thick at each end. Use a backsaw (tenon saw) and a chisel to remove the waste, as shown. Next cut the two pieces of 1 x ⁹⁄₁₆ in. (25 x 15 mm) softwood lipping to length and glue and screw them to the bottom of the rails using the 1 in. (25 mm) x No. 6 gauge screws. Wipe away any excess glue before it has a chance to dry, and assemble the rails to the head and footboard assemblies.

The two lines transferred in step 1 enable you to line up the bolts with the tenons. Find the center of the legs and drill two holes evenly spaced with the ¼ in. (6 mm) bit. Drill through the leg, through the tenon, and into the rail, keeping the drill square to the leg. Use measuring tape as a depth gauge on the bit so that you only drill the length of the bolts. Repeat this process on the other three legs.

Once the bed is assembled you will now have to insert the cylindrical nuts for the bunk-bed bolts. This can be a little tricky to get right because, no matter how careful you have been to keep your drill square in step 6, some error will almost certainly have occurred. For ease of explanation, this step is shown in more detail. Insert the bolts into the holes, leaving about 1 ³⁄₁₆ in. (30 mm) protruding. Use a square or a straightedge to sight the top and bottom of each bolt, then draw two sets of parallel lines and make a mark across them about ³⁄₈ in. (10 mm) short of the length of the bolts. Drill a ⁵⁄₁₆ in. (8 mm) hole through this mark to receive the cylindrical nut. Insert the nuts and screw up the bolts, but be careful not to over tighten them at this stage.

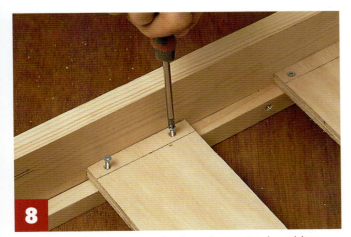

Cut the plywood slats to the length required and lay them across the two pieces of lipping. Pre-drill and countersink each one, then glue and screw them into place using two ¹¹⁄₁₆ in. (18 mm) x No. 6 screws at both ends of each slat. The end slats should be 2 in. (50 mm) from the headboard and footboard, with a 4 in. (100 mm) gap between all the others.

TIP

When drilling the holes for the bunk-bed bolts in the legs, you will find it easier and more efficient if you place the bed on the floor with one end pressed up against a wall.

Jewelry Box

Making boxes is a great way to use up small amounts of lumber, and there are lots of interesting ways to decorate and personalize a box. This small jewelry box is made from American ash, which is a very pale lumber. The corners are decorated with spline dovetails made from bog oak, which is ancient lumber that has been immersed in a bog for hundreds of years and has consequently turned jet black. However, any two contrasting lumbers will work equally well. To insert the splines, you will need to make a simple jig on which to run your router.

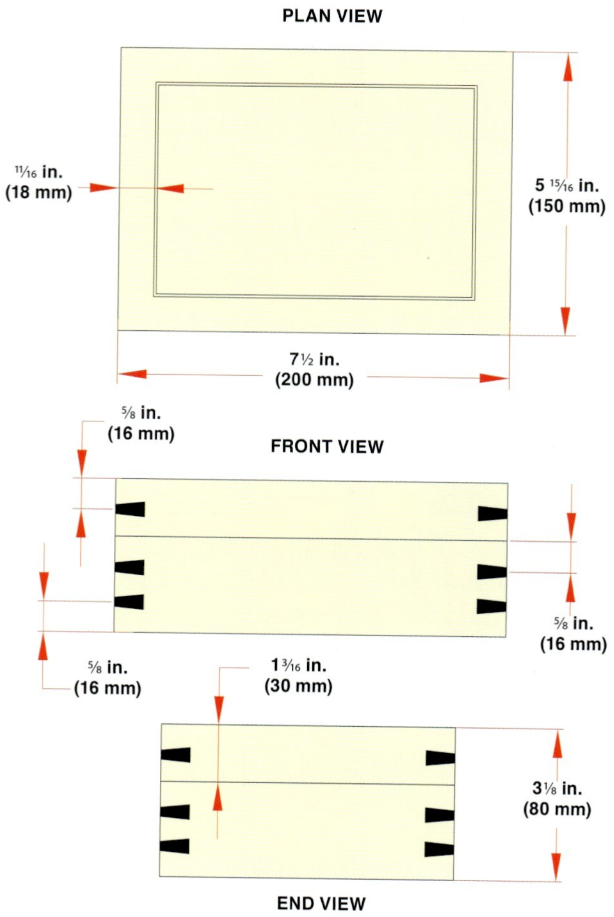
PLAN VIEW
11/16 in.
(18 mm)
5 15/16 in.
(150 mm)
7 1/2 in.
(200 mm)
5/8 in.
(16 mm)
FRONT VIEW
5/8 in.
(16 mm)
5/8 in.
(16 mm)
1 3/16 in.
(30 mm)
3 1/8 in.
(80 mm)
END VIEW

Essential Tools & Materials

Tools

- measuring and marking tools
- miter saw
- backsaw (tenon saw)
- flexible pullsaw
- hacksaw
- band clamp
- bench vise
- hammer
- power sander (optional)
- F- or G-clamps
- screwdriver
- router, router table, small dovetail cutter 5/16 in. (8 mm) in diameter, straight cutter 1/4 in. (6 mm)

Hardware etc.

- glue
- panel pins, 1/2 in. (12 mm)
- sandpaper
- piano hinge

Wood

- 2 pieces 7 7/8 x 3 1/8 x 11/16 in. (200 x 80 x 18 mm) American ash (side)
- 2 pieces 5 15/16 x 3 1/8 x 11/16 in. (150 x 80 x 18 mm) American ash (side)
- approx. 6 11/16 x 4 15/16 x 1/2 in. (170 x 125 x 12 mm) American ash (top)
- approx. 7 1/16 x 5 1/8 x 1/4 in. (180 x 130 x 6 mm) plywood or MDF (base)
- 14 x 1 9/16 x 1/2 in. (350 x 40 x 12 mm) bog oak (spline dovetails)
- 14 3/16 x 7 7/8 x 11/16 in. (360 x 200 x 18 mm) MDF (jig top plate)
- 7 1/6 x 4 x 11/16 in. (180 x 100 x 18 mm) MDF
- 4 x 4 x 11/16 in. (100 x 100 x 18 mm) MDF

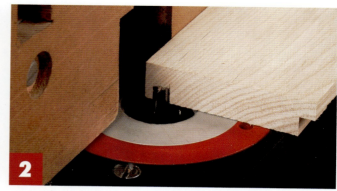

1 Prepare the lumber. Ideally, have one length of lumber that can be cut up to make all four sides. This makes it easy to machine. Select a well-figured piece for use on the top. Take the length of lumber for the sides and mark the thickness of the top on it. Mark the rabbet for the base panel. This should be ¼ in. (6 mm) wide and ⅜ in. (10 mm) high.

2 Using the router table, cut a groove ¼ in. (6 mm) wide by ³⁄₁₆ in. (10 mm) deep just inside the line that you marked for the top. Also machine the rabbet for the base panel.

3 When the routing is complete, cut the sides to length using a miter saw. Roughly assemble the sides and measure the size of the top into the grooves. The top panel should be cut to be a little undersized across the grain, to allow for any expansion.

4 Fit the straight cutter in the router table and machine a rabbet around the edge of the top panel. The height of the cutter should be set to produce a tongue ¼ in. (6 mm) thick to fit the groove, and the width should be set to produce an even space around the top panel when it is assembled in the frame. This may involve a certain amount of trial and error, so set a narrow width to start with and increase it as necessary.

◄ Lay out the components of the box (base and four sides), ready for assembly.

5

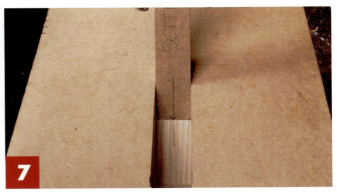

Fit the top panel into the grooves in the sides and, being careful not to get any glue on it, glue all the miter joints. Clamp the assembly using a band clamp, and make sure that the top panel is centrally positioned. Make a jig for the insertion of the spline dovetails (see Making the Jig).

Mark out the position of the splines as shown in the drawing. Use the setting bar on the jig to align the center of the slot with the marked line. Clamp the box in position and secure the whole assembly in the bench vise.

Making the Jig

To support the router and guide it through the corners accurately, a jig is needed. It must be made to suit your router. This version was made to fit a router with a $^{15}/_{16}$ in. (24 mm) guidebush.

The jig components are made from $^{11}/_{16}$ in. (18 mm) MDF, though plywood would do equally well. Begin by cutting the top plate to size. Mark the center of the board, and rout out a recess that exactly matches your guidebush. Use the side fence to guide the router and a straight cutter to make narrow passes until the recess is just wide enough to contain the guidebush without any play. Don't worry if the recess is slightly off-center.

The frame below the top plate consists of four components. Make sure that the angle between the supports is exactly 90° and that the top plate sits on it at precisely 45°. The boards do not need to be as wide as the top plate: 4 in. (100 mm) should be adequate.

Once the boards have been cut to length and mitered, cut a slot in the mitered ends—make it the same width as the guidebush and about 1 $^9/_{16}$ in. (40 mm) long. This is where the cutter will pass through the side of the box, so you need good clearance.

Glue and screw the jig tightly together. Pre-drill the MDF to avoid splitting the core, and countersink the screws so that they won't foul up the router.

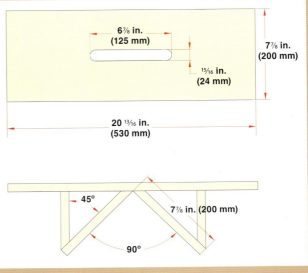

6 $^7/_8$ in. (125 mm)

7 $^7/_8$ in. (200 mm)

$^{15}/_{16}$ in. (24 mm)

20 $^{13}/_{16}$ in. (530 mm)

45°

7 $^7/_8$ in. (200 mm)

90°

8

Fit the router with the dovetail cutter and the guidebush. Place it on the jig, and with the power off, center it over the box and plunge the cutter so that it just touches the top of the corner. Lock it down and then set the depth stop to make a pass about 3/8 in. (10 mm) deeper than this. Release the router and pull it back to the front of the slot. Plunge the machine to the depth you have set and engage the plunge lock. Start the motor and run it gently along the slot, cutting through the corner of the box. Move slowly to ensure that you make a clean cut without causing any breakout as the cutter exits the lumber. Turn off the router without releasing the plunge lock, and once the motor has stopped, lift it out of the jig, reset the jig on the next line, and repeat the procedure until all the corners have been machined.

9

Once you have routed all four corners, the box is ready for the splines. To make the splines, fit the router in the router table and use the dovetail cutter again. You are aiming to make one long length, which can then be cut up to fit in the routed slots.

10

Set the dovetail cutter as shown, just protruding past the fence, so it makes a shallow cut. Make a pass on each side of the board and then check the fit in the routed slots. Reset the fence a fraction farther back and make another pass if the lumber is too large. Continue this process until the spline is a tight fit in the slot. Ideally, it should be tapped in with a hammer. When you are happy with the fit, saw off the molded edge of the board and cut into short lengths.

11

◀ Check the fit of the splines. Cut the splines roughly to length and glue in position. Once the glue has dried, trim off the end of the splines with the pullsaw. If you do not have one, a backsaw (tenon saw) may be used, but be careful not to damage the side of the box. Finally, sand down the splines with a power sander, or use a sanding block.

12 Carefully cut the base of the box to size so that it is a snug fit in the rabbet. Apply a little glue to the rabbet and pin the base in place with panel pins.

13 It is now time to cut off the top of the box. Mark a line around the box, in pencil, exactly 1 3/16 in. (30 mm) down from the top. Set the box on its side on the workbench and secure it with the F- or G-clamp. Take the backsaw (tenon saw) and carefully work around the line, turning the box as you go.

14 Once the lid has been parted, take a piece of sandpaper and clamp it to the workbench. Smooth the edges of both the box and the lid to remove any unevenness, until both parts fit neatly together.

15 The final job is to attach the hinge. There are many different types of hinge that you could use, but probably the easiest to fit is the piano hinge. These hinges are available in a variety of lengths, but you will probably need to trim it to length using a hacksaw. The hinge should be positioned with the knuckle protruding out of the back of the box. Mark the position of the hinge on the back of the box and cut a shallow rabbet on this line using the router table.

◄ The rabbet should be deep enough to accommodate the thickness of the hinge leaf plus the attaching screw. Screw the hinge in place.

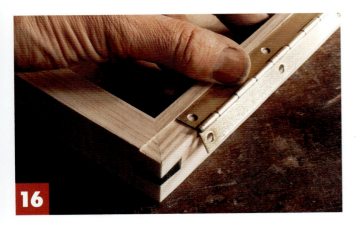

16

Tall Storage Chest

This project takes the weekend carpenter on to the next level: simple cabinet-making. To construct the drawers it is best to use a professional, full-size dovetail jig; however, smaller jigs with a cutting width of up to 11 13/16 in. (300 mm) are also available. Look for rigidity in the plate, and ensure that the guidebush will fit your router. The jig should be mounted on a plywood or MDF base, with a 1 in. (25 mm) hole drilled to a depth of 1 in. (25 mm) in one overhanging end to receive the protruding cutter when not being used for machining. The front of the drawer is placed face down on the top of the jig, with the relevant side mounted vertically in place. The offset, which enables the pins and sockets of the dovetail to align, is achieved by using a small pin that screws into the side of the jig.

If you do not have access to a good-quality table saw and planer, get the lumbers prepared to size at a yard or joinery shop. You could use ash, which is probably the cheapest hardwood. However, it tends to tear along the grain, so keep your tools perfectly honed, and expect to spend some time later finishing with the cabinet scraper.

Essential Tools & Materials

Tools

- pencil
- steel ruler or measuring tape
- square
- marking knife
- coping saw
- drill with 1/8 in. (3 mm) and 3/16 in. (4 mm) twist bits, countersink bit
- circular saw (or table saw)
- router with 1/4 in. (6 mm) straight cutter and 45-degree bevel cutter, dovetail cutting jig and 7/16 in. (11 mm) dovetail cutter
- biscuit jointer, 28 size 10 and 50 size 20 biscuits
- range of bevel-edge chisels
- jack plane
- block plane
- cabinet scraper
- framing clamps
- sash clamps or clamp heads
- workbench with vise
- power hand plane (optional)

Hardware etc.

- 35 countersink screws 2 in. (50 mm) x No. 8
- 4 countersink screws 1 in. (25 mm) x No. 8
- 6 chrome or brushed steel handles
- 9/16 in. (15 mm) molding pins
- PVA wood glue
- sandpaper in grits 120 to 400

Wood

- 14 pieces 15 1/8 x 1 5/8 x 3/4 in. (385 x 43 x 20 mm) hardwood, mitered at both ends (side runners)
- 14 pieces 18 1/2 x 1 5/8 x 3/4 in. (470 x 43 x 20 mm) hardwood, mitered at both ends (front and back runners)
- 2 pieces 39 x 15 9/16 x 3/4 in. (990 x 396 x 20 mm hardwood (sides)
- 21 5/8 x 17 1/8 x 3/4 in. (550 x 436 x 20 mm) hardwood (top)
- 18 1/2 x 4 x 3/4 in. (470 x 100 x 20 mm) hardwood (false plinth)
- 6 pieces 18 x 4 15/16 x 3/4 in. (458 x 125 x 20 mm) hardwood (drawer fronts)
- 12 pieces 14 3/8 x 4 15/16 x 1/2 in. (365 x 125 x 12 mm) hardwood (drawer sides)
- 6 pieces 17 7/8 x 4 5/16 x 1/2 in. (454 x 111 x 12 mm) hardwood (drawer backs)
- 6 pieces 18 1/4 x 14 x 1/4 in. (463 x 350 x 6 mm) plywood (drawer bottoms)
- 19 7/8 x 38 3/16 x 1/4 in. (505 x 970 x 6 mm) plywood (chest back)
- 12 pieces 2 1/2 x 3/4 x 1/4 in. (65 x 20 x 6 mm) plywood waste pieces (drawer stops)

Tall Storage Chest

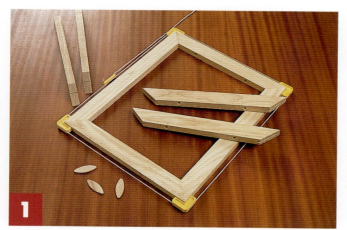

◀ Prepare the lumber as per the cutting list; cut the top and sides to length and biscuit-joint them along the edges. Arrange all the miter-cut runners on edge, with the shorter edge uppermost. Make a mark across the end grain ¾ in. (20 mm) away from the short point at both ends, as shown: use one of the runners as a guide stick, hold it in place across all the miters, and then mark along the underside with a pencil. On the shorter side runners, mark and drill two ³⁄₁₆ in. (4 mm) diameter countersunk holes, 2 in. (50 mm) in from the short point of the miters. Sort the runners into seven sets of four, two sides and a front and back, and cut a slot into the edge of the miters for a size 10 biscuit, using the end-grain mark as a register mark for the jointer. Ensure that the work is securely clamped or that you screw the jointer to the workbench and use a fixed stop. The small amount of breakout on the short point, where the end of the biscuit will show, will not be seen and can be removed with a coping saw later.

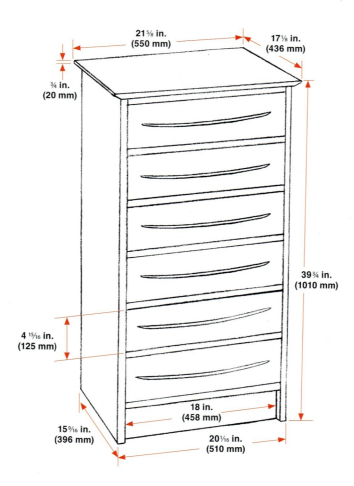

21⅝ in.
(550 mm)

17⅛ in.
(436 mm)

¾ in.
(20 mm)

39¾ in.
(1010 mm)

4¹⁵⁄₁₆ in.
(125 mm)

18 in.
(458 mm)

15⁹⁄₁₆ in.
(396 mm)

20¹⁄₁₆ in.
(510 mm)

2 Glue and clamp each frame, lay it flat with all glue wiped off, and ensure that it is perfectly square before leaving to dry.

◄ When dry, release the frames and number them 1 to 7 on the back edge with each frame's best face up. Check that they are uniform, and if necessary plane the outer edges until they are all the same width and all square to the front edge. Stack the frames, ensuring that they are flat and level. Cut 12 waste pieces of plywood into small trapezia to form drawer stops. Glue and pin them in place to the six lower frames, with the front edge of the plywood back ¾ in. (20 mm) from the front edge of the frame, i.e. the thickness of the drawer fronts.

◄ This picture shows two drawer fronts mounted face down in the dovetail jig, with the thinner sides clamped face in. Ensure that the parts are cut perfectly square and the side is flush to the upper face of the front. When you place the fronts in position, check that what will be the top edge of the drawer will have a pin and not a socket. Adjust this by moving the work to the left or right.

5 Mount the guidebush that comes with the template on the underside of your router, push the plunger down, and lock it off. Insert the dovetail bit and adjust the depth to ⁷⁄₁₆ in. (11 mm). Be careful not to inadvertently release the plunge lock when setting the fine depth adjuster, or when you finish a pass—if you do, especially when the router is running, you will ruin both cutter and guidebush.

Insert the dovetail template in place, using the adjustment nuts to achieve an exact alignment of the cutting line on the template surface with the join between the front and side parts of the drawer, and start to machine. Always work from left to right, allowing the router to achieve full speed prior to entry, and make the cuts through both pieces of lumber.

This picture shows clearly a fully machined joint still clamped in the jig and an exploded joint that demonstrates how the workpieces should look when you have finished the cut.

8

9

To cut a groove for the drawer bottoms, fit a ¼ in. (6 mm) straight cutter to your router and set the depth of cut to ³⁄₁₆ in. (10 mm), with the distance on the fence ⁵⁄₁₆ in. (8 mm) in from the bottom edge of the drawer sides and fronts. These grooves or housings should stop short on both ends of the front by ³⁄₁₆ in. (10 mm). Square off the end of these housings with a ¼ in. (6 mm) chisel. The sides can be routed the full length, since the housing will fall in line with the lowest socket, provided you have mounted the fronts correctly in the jig (see step 4).

While the router is set up, rout out the carcass sides for the plywood back at this stage. As before, cut a ¼ in. (6 mm) groove ³⁄₁₆ in. (10 mm) deep, but this time adjust the fence to cut ³⁄₁₆ in. (10 mm) in from the rear edge. Run the groove the entire length of both sides. Take care that the fence is parallel at the start and finish of each pass.

10

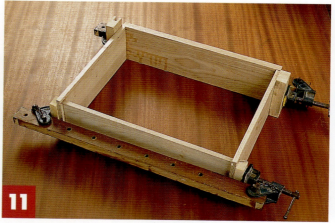

11

Cut a housing to the same depth, ½ in. (12 mm) wide, taken ⅜ in. (10 mm) in from the end of the drawer sides and stopped at the ¼ in. (6 mm) housing for the drawer bottom. You can either use a ½ in. (12 mm) straight cutter or make two passes with the ¼ in. (6 mm) one. Clamp a guide batten across the lumber or use the router's fence across the end of the drawer side—the latter is far quicker, but take extreme care that the router doesn't "rock in" when starting the cut. Cabinet-scrape and sand all the inner faces of the drawers.

Glue up the drawers upside down. This allows you to check the positioning of the drawer back, and in addition will stop the back from sliding down the housing. Note that the glue blocks are pulled back from the drawer front to allow the dovetails to pull up tightly.

12

When fitting the bottoms to the drawers, you may need to use a block plane to achieve a slight bevel on the underside of the plywood. Glue each bottom in the grooves and pin the back edge to the underside of the drawer back. Stack all the drawers interspersed with the frames on a level surface, check for any errors, especially on the width of the drawers, and rectify as required. No drawer should be narrower than the frames—if they are, you will once again have to plane the widths of the frames. Number the drawers on the back.

13

Lay one side down on the bench and, starting at the top, mark the position of each frame and drawer, ensuring that they are square to the front edge of the side. Run a bead of glue where the frames lie, use a ⅛ in. (3 mm) drill bit to start the screws, and screw the six lower frames in place. Turn the assembly over and lay it on the other side of the carcass.

14

Repeat step 12 for the other side, checking continually that the carcass doesn't shift to a parallelogram. When satisfied, leave out to dry, lying on its back. Use a bevel cutter with a guide wheel to bevel the underside edge of the top. Cut to a depth of ⁹⁄₁₆ in. (14 mm) on the front and both sides, leaving the back edge as is. Place the top on the carcass and center it, which should leave a ¾ in. (20 mm) overhang all around. Mark the position of the top frame from the inside of the carcass. Glue and screw the final frame to the top, making sure that the front overhang is correctly positioned. Replace the top on the carcass and screw and glue top in place via the frame sides.

15

Fit each drawer to its opening, planing the sides of the drawer where necessary and using a block plane to round the rear ends of each drawer side. Use a piece of thin cardboard to achieve a consistent gap all the way around the drawer front. Fit the handles; insert and pin the back as for the drawer bottoms. Screw the false plinth using two blocks set back 1⁹⁄₁₆ in. (40 mm) from the front edge of the carcass.

Privacy Screen

A privacy screen is normally thought of as three or four panels connected by hinges. However, you can use as many panels as you wish—this one has 24, connected together with rope, based on an idea I (PG) saw in Bali. This project is best completed with the help of a router table, a useful addition to the home workshop that turns your router into a small spindle molder. It will speed up the tedious part of this project and should ensure greater accuracy in the fit of the male and female profiles.

You can use almost any lumber—a maple or sycamore screen with stainless steel cleats would look very stylish, if somewhat on the extravagant side. When selecting the lumber at a yard, be firm in refusing any length that is twisted or warped, or has dry knots on either edge.

For the finish use an interior color wash to which you can add a small amount of gold powder, available in art shops. The tassels used to hide the ends of the nylon ropes have a wooden flange on the top, through which the nylon is threaded and is then tied off under the body of the tassel.

Essential Tools & Materials

Tools
- pencil
- measuring tape
- square
- screwdriver
- backsaw (tenon saw)
- jigsaw
- electric drill, ¼ in. (6 mm) extra-long multi-speed bit, ¼ in. (6 and 7 mm) twist bits, ½ in. (12 mm) flat bit
- block plane
- large sash clamp or clamp heads
- router mounted on router table, half-round cutter ¼ in. (6 mm) radius, ogee cutter ¼ in. (6 mm) radius
- workbench

Hardware etc.
- ³⁄₁₆ in. (10 mm) diameter nylon rope, 30 ft. (9 m) long
- 3 small plastic cleats (these last two items can be bought in a marine supply or surf/dive shop)
- 6 screws 1 in. (25 mm) x No. 6
- sandpaper in grits 80, 100, and 120

Wood
- 24 pieces 1 x 2 ¹⁵⁄₁₆ x 63 in. (25 x 75 x 1600 mm) straight-grained pine or similar (S4S)

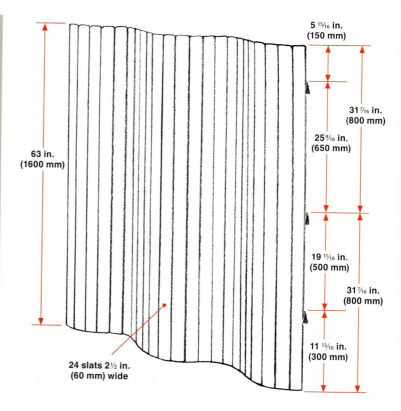

63 in. (1600 mm)

5 ¹⁵⁄₁₆ in. (150 mm)

31 ⁷⁄₁₆ in. (800 mm)

25 ⁹⁄₁₆ in. (650 mm)

19 ¹¹⁄₁₆ in. (500 mm)

31 ⁷⁄₁₆ in. (800 mm)

11 ¹³⁄₁₆ in. (300 mm)

24 slats 2½ in. (60 mm) wide

Although this project uses modern nylon rope and cleats, and the joining profiles have been adapted for use with a standard router cutter or spindle molder, it is essentially the same design that has been used for hundreds of years in the Far East. Older screens of this type would have been made of what was then a plentiful supply of hardwood, but pine or a similar softwood will do just as well.

1 Cut 24 lengths of lumber to 63 in. (1.6 m) long. Mark each length with a corresponding number (from 1 to 24) and mark a top. Number 1 will be the left-hand-side plank; make a mark on the edge halfway down, i.e. at 31 $\frac{7}{16}$ in. (800 mm). Make a further mark 5 $\frac{15}{16}$ in. (150 mm) from the top, and another 11 $\frac{13}{16}$ in. (300 mm) from the base, ensuring that these marks are in the center of the edge. Use a square to transfer these marks to the other edge. Clamp all the planks together, edge uppermost, and transfer the marks from plank 1 to all the others. Turn the pack over and repeat. Secure plank 1 in your vise and drill three $\frac{1}{2}$ in. (12mm) holes $\frac{1}{2}$ in. (12mm) deep to conceal the initial knots of the ropes, as shown here.

3 Fit a $\frac{1}{4}$ in. (6mm) radius ovolo cutter to your router, then mount the router in the router table. Use a scrap piece to set the fence in position. Depending on the type of table you are using, the fence, in all probability, will be set at a slight angle across the center of the cutter. The height of the cut should be to the centerline of the lumber's edge, and the thickness should be so you just skim the center edge with the cutter. The uppermost part of the profile should just touch the centerline drawn across the edge of each plank

2 Use a $\frac{1}{4}$ in. (6 mm) extra-long bit to drill the holes through which the rope will pass in plank 1. Drill halfway through, keeping the bit square to the lumber at all times, then drill from the other edge. If you find a slight misalignment, correct this with a small round file. A pillar drill or drill stand will speed up this process. Drill three $\frac{1}{4}$ in. (6mm) holes in the remaining planks.

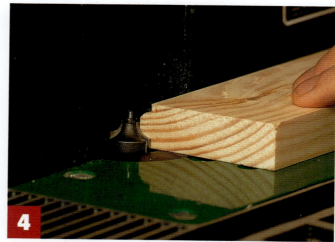

4 To achieve the profile, you need to make two passes, turning the lumber over after the first cut, as shown. When you are sure that the profile is correct, cut the edge of plank 1 that does not have the $\frac{1}{2}$ in. (12mm) holes drilled; this should be to the right-hand side of the plank. Then cut all the other planks on the right-hand side, except plank 24, which should be left square on the right-hand side.

5 To shape the tops, use a coin about ¾ in. (20 mm) in diameter and place it so that it touches the top edge and the reveal of the ovolo cut. Draw around it. Place the coin against the edge and the top on the other edge, and mark. Using a jigsaw, cut square through the ovolo profile to the lines. Change the cutter in the router to a half-round with a ¼ in. (6 mm) radius. Again, use a test piece to position the fence and the height of the cutter, then make the cut as shown.

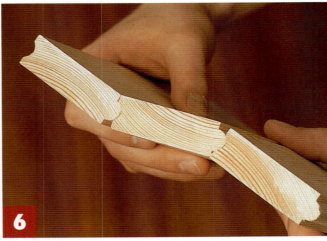

6 This shows in detail how the two profiles should match. Pass the left-hand side of all planks, except plank 1, through the router. Lay all the planks in order on the workbench.

7 Cut the rope into three equal lengths. Nylon rope will fray at the ends unless taped or fused. The best method is to fuse the ends together with the flame from a lighter. Make a clean cut while the rope is held taut. Take the new end and twist the rope in the direction that it falls. Run the flame of a lighter under the rope about 2 in. (50 mm) away from the end you are holding. Rotate the rope around and move the lighter over a ¾ in. (20 mm) section. As soon as you can see the outer surface fusing together, remove the flame and cool the rope in water.

TIP

If you are in any doubt whatsoever as to your competence in fusing the rope as demonstrated in step 7, you can also get a good result by taping the ends with electrical tape.

TIP

When routing the planks, take it slowly and keep a firm pressure downward. You may find it easier to enlist the help of an assistant to draw the planks from you as they come off the table.

8 Make a new cut in the middle of the section you have fused together. This process needs to be done at both ends of all three ropes. Tie a figure-eight knot at one end to act as a stopper in the ½ in. (12 mm) holes in plank 1.

9 Starting from plank 1, thread each rope through one plank at a time. Twist the rope with the lay, and if you find a hole tight, ream it out with a ¼ in. (6 mm) drill bit. Push each plank up tight as you work.

10 Use a large sash clamp to pull the planks together. Screw a plastic cleat just under each hole, pulling the ropes as tight as you can, and lock them off in the cleats. Offer up the tassels, if used; cut and fuse the ropes to the shortest possible length, then place the tassels in position, fixing them with glue or cotton binding.

Projects for the Bathroom

78 Vanity

86 Toilet Roll Holder and Towel Ring

87 Toothbrush and Mug Holder

88 Soap Dish

89 Duckboard

Vanity

This design, influenced by the English Arts and Crafts and the French Art Nouveau movements, is a joint effort with my (PG) wife, Liza, who made the ceramic basin and moldings. Although it is not a project for the beginner, providing your marking out is done with care, you should be able to produce a good-looking unit. Any reasonably stable hardwood can be used, although oak is the most stylistically correct for this type of design. The finish is a light coat of liming wax followed by a rich coat of beeswax.

When drawing out the shapes, take care that you do not make the curves too abrupt or too deep. Each curve should flow into the next. Achieving a balance for the upstand or backsplash is very much a matter of trial and error. The return curves at the rear of the top have to balance with the outer edge of the upstand. The best method is to cut a template as shown on page 222; place this on the top and look hard at how the lines of the top and upstand intersect from every conceivable angle. The legs are splayed at 5 degrees from vertical—the front legs are splayed both out and forward, while the back legs only splay out.

Essential Tools & Materials

Tools

- pencil
- measuring tape
- square
- marking knife
- mortise gauge
- screwdriver
- crosscut saw
- jigsaw
- spokeshave
- belt sander
- electric drill, ³⁄₁₆ and ⅛ in. (5, 4, and 3 mm) wood bits, countersink bit
- router with ¼, ½, and 1 in. (6, 12, and 25 mm) straight cutters, plus a quarter-round cutter of ¾ in. (22 mm) diameter with a ¼ in. (6 mm) radius for the upper curve of the top and a 1 in. (25 mm) diameter ogee cutter with a ⅛ in. (3 mm) radius for the underside
- biscuit jointer and 10 size 20 biscuits
- range of bevel-edge chisels
- jack plane
- block plane
- cabinet scraper
- workbench
- sash clamps
- table-mounted circular saw (optional)
- electric hand plane (optional)
- band saw (optional)

Hardware etc.

- 4 brass countersink screws 2 in. (50 mm) x No. 10
- 18 brass roundhead screws ¹¹⁄₁₆ in. (18 mm) x No. 6
- 6 stretcher plates
- sandpaper in grits 100 to 400
- waterproof wood glue (Cascamite or similar)

Wood

- 4 pieces 33⁷⁄₁₆ x 2½ x 2½ in. (850 x 60 x 60 mm) American white oak (legs)
- 33⁷⁄₁₆ x 6 ¹¹⁄₁₆ x 1⅜ in. (850 x 170 x 35 mm) American white oak (front rail)
- 2 pieces 16½ x 6 ¹¹⁄₁₆ x 1⅜ in. (420 x 170 x 35 mm) American white oak (side rails)
- 27½ x 4 x ¾ in. (700 x 100 x 20 mm) American white oak (rear rail)
- 106⁵⁄₁₆ (3 x 35⁷⁄₁₆) x 7⅞ x ¾ in. (2700 [3 x 900] x 200 x 20 mm) American white oak (top)
- 31⁷⁄₁₆ x 4 x ¾ in. (800 x 100 x 20 mm) American white oak (upstand)

Plane the legs true, 2½ in. (60 mm) square and 33⁷⁄₁₆ in. (850 mm) long. When selecting the face and face-edge marks, bear in mind that the legs will splay out, so use the grain pattern to accentuate this if possible. If you use an electric plane, as shown here, never plane closer than about ¹⁄₆₄ in. (0.5 mm) from the finished line, and keep your hand well away from the blades. Always finish with a jack plane, as this gives greater control and a far superior finish.

Select the legs according to grain type and direction for the best location, front or back pair, and mark accordingly. For the front pair, mark an 85-degree compound bevel with the lowest point being the front outer corner. For the rear legs, mark a simple bevel with the lower portion on the outer faces. For the front rail mortise, mark ½ in. (12 mm) with a mortise gauge ⁷⁄₁₆ in. (11.5 mm) in from the front face. Cut all eight mortises using a router with a ½ in. (12 mm) straight cutter, except for the two inner faces of the back legs; these are cut to ¼ in. (6 mm) wide and ⁹⁄₃₂ in. (7 mm) in from the rear face. Set the depth of cut to maximum—using standard straight cutters this is 1³⁄₁₆ in. (30 mm), and is just about sufficient.

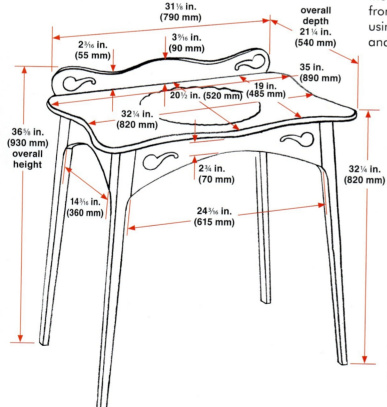

TIP

Longer straight cutters, called pocket cutters, are available for cutting deeper mortises.

Do not use steel or brass-plated screws in oak, as they cause severe discoloration of the lumber; instead, use solid brass screws. Always cut the screw hole with a steel screw of the same size first, withdraw the steel screw and replace with a brass one.

◄ Here the front left leg is being marked for the curve between the upper end of the taper and the shoulder line of the front rail on the inner face. Repeat these markings on the front face and then for the other three legs. (The back legs should be marked on the inner and rear faces.)

4 The taper is marked out as in the diagram on page 222—remember that the upper thickness, from where the curve springs, is 1 9/16 in. (40 mm). Make sure that the marks are on the proscribed faces, otherwise you will remove one set of marks when you cut the tapers.

To remove the waste from the legs, use a jigsaw with the work mounted. Move the leg along the workbench as you proceed, to ensure you do not bind the saw blade. After the first cut, rotate the leg through 90 degrees and use the non-parallel jaws of the workbench to secure the job. Do not cut close to the line, especially when negotiating the curve—no matter how good the jigsaw, a small amount of wander on the blade is inevitable. If you have access to a bandsaw, use it for this step.

Any error in the cut of the inner faces of the legs can be removed with a spokeshave or a belt sander, using the "nose" of the tool to finish the curve.

7 Mount the legs in a vise or workbench and plane the inside corner down to the 1 3/8 in. (35 mm marks). This will leave a triangle reminiscent of a Gothic arch. Draw a line joining the two 1 3/8 in. (35 mm) marks across the face of the triangle and use a belt sander to remove the lumber up to the line. The curved triangle that will result should be continued down the inner corner of the leg, feathering out about 4 in. (100 mm) below the shoulder lines. Mount each leg vertically in the vise and remove the end-grain waste down to the bevel marks, the bulk with the belt sander, finishing off with a block plane. Finish all faces of the legs with a cabinet scraper.

◀ Cut the four rails to the sizes on page 78—these are overlong, but will be cut to the correct length when the leg bevels have been marked. For the front rail, mark 24 3/16 in. (615 mm) along the upper edge, then lay the sliding bevel, set to 85 degrees, on the lower edge and mark with a knife. Slide the bevel along the length of the tenons—1 3/16 in. (30 mm) unless you have cut the leg mortises deeper—and mark another line at each end. Square all lines around the rail, using the bevel and a square. Repeat for the smaller section rear rail. The side rails are 14 3/16 in. (360 mm) shoulder to shoulder, with the difference that the rear shoulder will be square to the upper edge; add the length of the tenons and cut to size. Clamp a batten parallel to the shoulder offset by the distance of the edge of your router to the edge of a 1 in. (25 mm) straight cutter, and remove the cheeks of the tenons.

9 Cut away the excess portions—for the large tenons, 1 3/8 in. (35 mm) from the top and 3/4 in. (20 mm) from the bottom; for the smaller tenons on the rear rail, 1 in. (25 mm) from the top and 3/4 in. (20 mm) from the bottom. The measurements are taken from the shoulder line and are marked at 90 degrees to the shoulder, not the edge. Round off the edges of the tenons to fit the mortises, clean up the shoulders, and assemble.

◀ Once you have a good fit with all the shoulders meeting the legs, mark the top of the rails to replicate the bevels on the legs, disassemble and plane in the vise, checking the angle by using the sliding bevel. Before disassembling, make a small mark where the curve of each leg meets the adjacent rail. Once the top bevels have been planed, mark the center of the front and side faces, measure down 2 3/4 in. (70 mm) for the front and 2 15/16 in. (75 mm) for the sides, and mark. Use a long steel ruler to achieve a smooth curve between the three points. Draw the curve with a pencil then remove the waste with a jigsaw. Reassemble and check that the flow of the leg curves into the rails and that the top bevel is flat all the way across the table. Cut six slow wedges from scrap and glue up, as shown. Don't place the clamp higher than shown, or you may shear the short grain on the curve of rail where it meets the leg. Tighten all clamps, check that the interior is square, and clean up.

11 Cut the three parts for the top to 35 7/16 in. (900 mm). Arrange them side by side, with the grain cupped alternately to minimize warping. Place any knots or defects in the center, where you will cut out for the basin. Biscuit-joint the pieces, glue up, and clamp together. When dry, place on the leg assembly with a ¾ in. (20 mm) overhang to the rear and sketch out the edge profile, using a soft pencil. To achieve perfect symmetry, draw one half, trace it, flip the tracing paper, and then press into the grain through the trace onto the other side with a hard pencil. Cut to the line with a jigsaw, smooth off with a belt sander, then rout the profile with a quarter-round cutter for the top edge and an ogee cutter for the bottom edge, leaving a small return of about ⅛ in. (3 mm) at the base.

12 Sketch out the profile of the upstand on a 31 7/16 x 4 in. (800 x 100 mm) scrap piece of MDF or plywood. Use the front edge of the top as a template, reducing the length by 11/16 in. (18 mm) at each end. Place the template in position and adjust your lines as required. When you are satisfied with the shape, cut it out with a jigsaw and look at it in place again. If you're unsure that each side is symmetrical, use the best end, mark the center, and flip the template over.

13 Transfer the template to the upstand (backsplash) and cut out. Drill four countersunk holes from the underside of the top to attach in place, but do not fit yet.

14 ◀ Lay the top upside down with the leg assembly in place and fit the stretcher plates in place. They will need to be bent slightly to accommodate the angled rails. Use only the slots that traverse the grain, because any expansion or contraction takes place across the width of lumber, not the length. Place the screws in the center of each slot. Turn upright, and screw and glue the upstand in place. Place the completed table on a flat, level surface, scribe around the base of each leg, and cut to the line with a backsaw (tenon saw). Then lay the ceramic basin upside down in place and draw round the rim, subtract the width of the rim, and draw a second inner circle; cut to this second line and fit the basin with a bead of silicone mastic.

Bathroom Accessories

These pieces are designed as a hardwood starter project. You need some basic skills, but not necessarily to have worked with hardwoods before. The project allows you to practice the skill of getting lumber perfectly flat and of an even thickness using hand tools. It also gives you practice with the cabinet scraper, an essential tool for obtaining a smooth surface on hardwoods. A biscuit jointer is used for the soap dish and the toothbrush holder; one can be rented for the weekend at a reasonable cost, although once you have used it and appreciated its time-saving versatility, you will probably want to purchase one.

Burr maple is used for the fittings and plain maple for the duckboard. Virtually any lumber could be used—see what your local lumberyard has in stock—but please don't use pine, because it is the quality of the lumber used that makes this set of accessories look so attractive. You must use water-resistant glue for this project, since all the items will be subject to the damp atmosphere of the bathroom. The finish is a natural beeswax polish.

Essential Tools & Materials

Tools
- pencil
- compasses
- measuring tape
- square
- crosscut saw
- jigsaw with scroll blade
- electric drill, ⅜ in. (10 mm), ¼ in. (6 mm) and ⅛ in. (3 mm) wood bits
- biscuit jointer and 5 size 20 biscuits
- coping saw
- half-round file
- ½ in. (12 mm) bevel-edge chisel
- jack plane
- block plane
- cabinet scraper
- workbench
- table-mounted circular saw (optional)

Hardware etc.
- sandpaper in grits 150 to 300
- water-resistant wood glue
- toothbrush mugs
- toilet roll holder
- towel ring

Wood
- 55⅛ x 4 x ¾ in. (1400 x 100 x 20 mm) burr maple or similar
- 492 x 1⅝ x ½ in. (12,500 x 42 x 13 mm) maple or similar
- 100 x ¼ in. (6 mm) dowel rods
- towel ring 6⅞ x 3⅜ x ¾ in. (175 x 86 x 20 mm)
- toilet roll holder 6⅞ x 3⅜ x ¾ in. (175 x 86 x 20 mm)
- soap dish 7¼ x 3⅜ x ¾ in. and 7¼ x 3⅜ x ¾ in. (185 x 86 x 20 mm and 185 x 86 x 20 mm)
- toothbrush and mug holder 11⁷⁄₁₆ x 3⁹⁄₁₆ x ¾ in. and 11⁷⁄₁₆ x 3⁹⁄₁₆ x ¾ in. (290 x 90 x 20 mm and 290 x 95 x 20 mm)
- duckboard 14 pieces 19⁵⁄₁₆ x 1⅝ x ½ in. (490 x 42 x 12 mm) and 4 pieces 22⁷⁄₁₆ x 1⅝ x ½ in. (570 x 42 x 12 mm)

Toilet Roll Holder and Towel Ring

1 Cut two lengths as per the wood list, then use a sharp jack plane to get the best face of your blocks perfectly flat. Once flat, plane the best edge true and square to the first face, then mark with face and edge marks. Set a marking gauge to ¾ in. (20 mm) and mark around the edges, then plane the other face down to the marks. Aim for fine shavings and plane with the direction of the grain at all times. When both faces are flat and parallel to each other, set your marking gauge to 3⅜ in. (86 mm), mark for the other edge, and plane down to that edge.

2 When the blocks are both accurately sized, use a block plane to remove the arris around the face sides. Take care that you do not cause splitting when you plane across the end grain; to avoid this, plane from both ends toward the center. You may find a sharp chisel the best method for the corners.

3 Finish off the front face with a cabinet scraper, then pre-drill pilot holes and screw on the fittings.

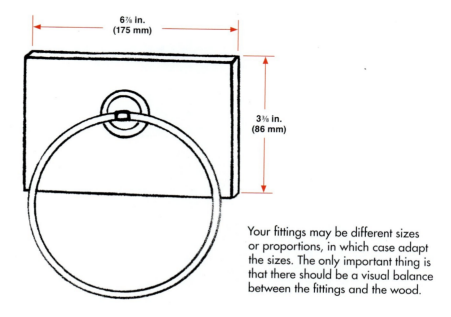

6⅞ in. (175 mm)

3⅜ in. (86 mm)

Your fittings may be different sizes or proportions, in which case adapt the sizes. The only important thing is that there should be a visual balance between the fittings and the wood.

Toothbrush and Mug Holder

Prepare the lumbers and mark out for the fittings. To determine the size of the holes for the tapered mugs, measure the diameters of the top and the base of the mug, halve the difference between the two diameters, and then add that figure to the base diameter. Draw the circles with a compass and drill a ⅜ in. (10 mm) hole in the center for the jigsaw scroll blade, shown here. Use a half-round file or rasp to clean up the jigsaw cut and to introduce the bevel needed to grip the mugs, as shown above. Take your time and test the fit of each mug as you go.

On the back piece, mark a line about 1 in. (25 mm) from the bottom and run this line along the length of the back. Lay the shelf part against the back and draw three lines on both sections; these will be used as registration marks for the biscuit jointer. One line needs to be in the center, and the other two should be approximately 2 in. (50 mm) in from each end. Use the biscuit jointer to cut the slots with the work held in the vise, shown here. Check for fit with the biscuits in place and then glue up.

TIP

When you are cutting a circular hole with a jigsaw, do not cut right up to the line. The blade can waver and you may make the cut too large on the underside.

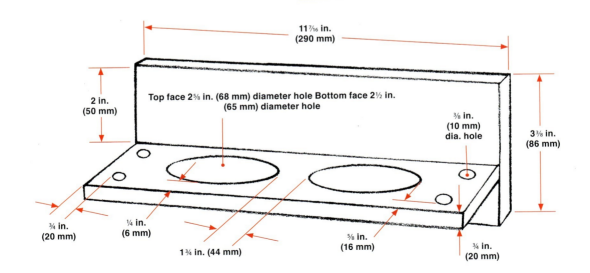

11⁷⁄₁₆ in. (290 mm)

2 in. (50 mm)

Top face 2⅝ in. (68 mm) diameter hole Bottom face 2½ in. (65 mm) diameter hole

⅜ in. (10 mm) dia. hole

3⅜ in. (86 mm)

¾ in. (20 mm)

¼ in. (6 mm)

1¾ in. (44 mm)

⅝ in. (16 mm)

¾ in. (20 mm)

Soap Dish

1 Prepare the lumber, then mark out the face side as shown here. The multiple lines on the wood are guides for the biscuit jointer to cut out the dish by means of multiple grooves. The lines that run across the width are to line up with the registration marks on the footplate of the jointer.

2 If you are nervous about cutting slots accurately, practice on scrap lumber first, and remember to travel in the direction of the blade, i.e. from left to right. Use the lines to keep the tool square, and never plunge the tool into the work until the blade has achieved full speed.

3

◄ The width of the dish allows you to use the end of a cabinet scraper to achieve a perfect finish—take care that the corners of the scraper do not cut into the sides of the dish. To fit the back in place, repeat step 2 as described for the toothbrush and mug holder, although this time you will only need two biscuits, owing to the shorter length of the soap dish.

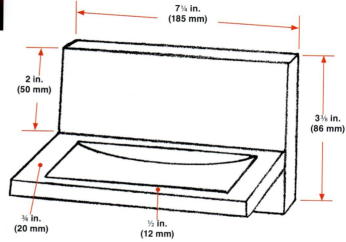

7¼ in. (185 mm)

2 in. (50 mm)

3⅜ in. (86 mm)

¾ in. (20 mm)

½ in. (12 mm)

Duckboard

1

Prepare all the lengths and lay out two long pieces with two short ones on top at the ends to make a frame. Get the four corners square and then clamp the pieces to the bench. To drill for the dowel rods, use a ¼ in. (6 mm) drill with a tape mark as a depth gauge, as shown. You do not want to drill all the way through both pieces, but stop the hole about halfway through the lower piece. Drill two holes on each corner and insert rods into the holes. The frame will now be rigid, allowing you to place the other slats equally spaced apart. Repeat the drilling at all points.

2

Cut off the protruding pegs with a coping saw, cutting as close as you can but taking care not to scratch the surface. Mark the planks then disassemble, keeping each rod in its correct hole. Glue up and clamp by using lengths of heavy lumber clamped at each end to make a sandwich.

3

Finally, use a sharp chisel to remove any excess glue from the pegs. You should finish the duckboard with a perfectly smooth surface, achieved by using the cabinet scraper.

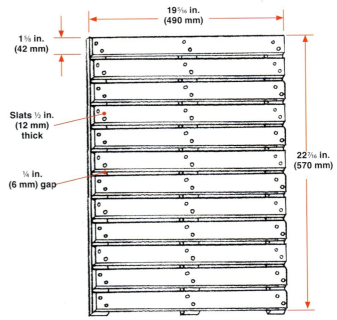

19⁵⁄₁₆ in. (490 mm)

1⅝ in. (42 mm)

Slats ½ in. (12 mm) thick

¼ in. (6 mm) gap

22⁷⁄₁₆ in. (570 mm)

Projects for the Living Room, Office, or Hall

92 Side Table

100 Console Table

120 Shoe Rack

126 Tray

104 Bookends

108 Table Lamp

114 Wastepaper Basket

132 Paneled Coffee Table

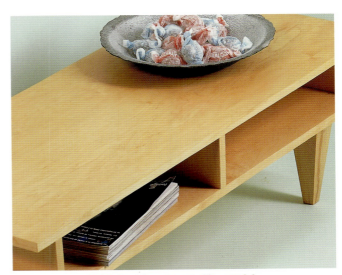

138 Modernist Coffee Table

Side Table

A simple side table can find a home in almost any room. This elegant design, with tapering legs and edge-molded top, is quick and easy to make, using simple jointing. To shape the legs, you will need to make a jig for use on the router table. As a finishing touch, you might want to try inlaying the top with a decorative line.

Essential Tools & Materials

Tools

- measuring and marking tools
- crosscut saw
- ripsaw
- biscuit jointer
- plane
- sander
- chisel
- electric drill, ³⁄₁₆ in. (4 mm) and countersink bits
- screwdriver
- clamps
- pair of toggle clamps
- router, router table, straight cutters ¼ in. (6 mm) and ¹⁄₁₆ in. (1.5 mm), bearing-guided chamfer cutter, bearing-guided profile cutter, inlay cutter

Hardware etc.

- Glue
- Screws: 4 x 1 in. (25 mm)
- sandpaper

Wood

- 4 pieces 25 x 1³⁄₁₆ x 1³⁄₁₆ in. (635 x 30 x 30 mm) English cherry (legs)
- 2 pieces 15³⁄₈ x 3⁹⁄₁₆ x ¾ in (390 x 90 x 19 mm) English cherry (rails)
- 2 pieces 10¼ x 3⁹⁄₁₆ x ¾ in. (260 x 90 x 19 mm) English cherry (rails)
- 20¹⁄₁₆ x 15 x ¾ in. (510 x 380 x 19 mm) English cherry (top)
- 10 pieces 1⁹⁄₁₆ x ¾ x ¾ in. (40 x 20 x 19 mm) cherry (buttons)
- 31⁷⁄₁₆ x 6¼ x ½ or ¹¹⁄₁₆ in. (800 x 160 x 12 or 18 mm) MDF (leg-tapering jig)
- 100 x ¹⁄₁₆ in. (2500 x 1.5 mm) stained boxwood (inlay line)

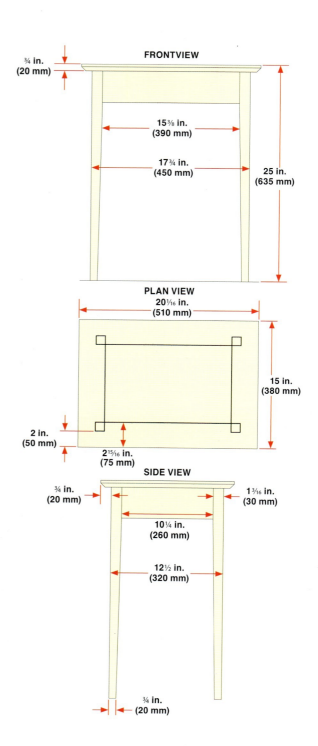

FRONT VIEW

¾ in. (20 mm)

15³⁄₈ in. (390 mm)

17¾ in. (450 mm)

25 in. (635 mm)

PLAN VIEW

20¹⁄₁₆ in. (510 mm)

15 in. (380 mm)

2 in. (50 mm)

2¹⁵⁄₁₆ in. (75 mm)

SIDE VIEW

¾ in. (20 mm)

1³⁄₁₆ in. (30 mm)

10¼ in. (260 mm)

12½ in. (320 mm)

¾ in. (20 mm)

1 Prepare the lumber for the frame and cut to length. The legs are left square at this stage. Biscuit joints will be used to assemble the frame because they are quick and easy to make. First, mark the position of the joints on the rails. They should be centrally placed, so set the combination square to 1¾ in. (45 mm).

2 Mark the legs. Keep the same setting on the combination square and measure down from the top. Remember to mark two adjacent faces.

3 Set the biscuit jointer so that the biscuit position is roughly located in the center of the board thickness, and cut all the joints on the rail ends. Clamp the rails securely to the workbench when machining them, and make sure that you hold the jointer level.

4 Before cutting the joints on the legs, raise the jointer fence by ³⁄₁₆ in. (10 mm). This will set the joint back to the middle of the leg and give a much better appearance.

5 Clamp the legs to the workbench and cut the joints.

6 The cutter used with the jig is a template profiler, which is a straight cutter with a bearing matching the diameter of the cutter mounted on the shank. The bearing is guided by the shape of the jig or template, so that the cutter will reproduce the shape.

7 Set the cutter height so that the bearing is running securely on the baseboard of the jig.

8 The fence should be set in line with the cutter bearing so that the body of the cutter is protected by it. Start the router and use the toggle clamps as handholds. Run the jig past the cutter and make a shallow pass. Take care because the cutter can plunge too deeply if you are not careful. Continue machining the edge until it is smooth. Roll the leg over in the jig and repeat the process. Remember to taper only the inside faces with the biscuit slots.

9 Once all the legs have been machined, the final job before assembling the frame is to cut a groove in the top of the rails. This is needed to locate the "buttons" that will be used to hold the top in position. Again use the router table and insert the ¼ in. (6 mm) straight cutter. This should be set with its outside edge about ¾ in. (19 mm) from the fence; its depth should be ³⁄₁₆ in. (10 mm). The grooves may all be cut in one pass. Make sure that you are machining the top inside face of each rail.

Tapered Leg Jig

The tapering jig is a useful workshop aid. It may be easily modified to cope with a variety of leg sizes and taper angles simply by resetting the guide battens. To taper the legs accurately, a special jig is needed. This can be made from a few pieces of MDF; the only hardware that you need is a pair of toggle clamps to hold the leg in position.

Start with the baseboard. One long edge must be perfectly straight and true in order for the cutter bearing to run against it. Refer to the picture and note how the jig is set out. You need one long batten, roughly 1 in. (25 mm) square and 24³⁄₁₆ in. (615 mm) or more long. You also need two short lengths of batten to use as end stops.

Mark the position of the long batten adjacent to the true straight edge; mark a point ¾ in. (20 mm) in from the edge close to one end of the baseboard. Now measure along the edge 20¼ in. (515 mm), and mark a point exactly 1³⁄₁₆ in. (30 mm) in. Draw a line between these two points and that is where the batten should be fixed. Place a short batten at the foot end and then put a leg blank into the jig. This must be cut exactly to length. Take the second short batten, butt it up tightly against the top of the leg, and screw into position.

Now simply fix the toggle clamps in suitable positions to hold the leg securely for routing. Make sure that they are set back so that they cannot come into contact with the cutter.

10 The frame components, ready for assembly.

11 Tackle the assembly in two stages. Start by gluing the two long rails and the legs. Apply the glue to the biscuit slots and then insert the biscuits. Put a little glue on the end of the rail and assemble the joints. Use just enough glue for a tiny amount to be squeezed out as the joint is assembled, but do not overdo it because this can cause problems when it comes to applying a finish to the table. Wipe away any surplus glue with a damp cloth.

12 Carefully clamp up both assemblies, making sure that the rails are flush with the tops of the legs, and set them aside to dry.

13 Once the glue has dried, finish the frame by fitting the cross rails. Stand the frame on a level surface when doing this and ensure that it is all square as you tighten the clamps. Compare the diagonal measurements from corner to corner—they must be exactly equal.

14 The top is made up from several boards biscuit-jointed together. It is then cut to size and the edge is molded with the bearing-guided chamfer cutter.

15 Do the molding in a series of passes. Always start on the end-grain and work around the board, finishing on the side grain; this prevents breakout. Keep making passes until you have a well-defined chamfer around the underside of the board.

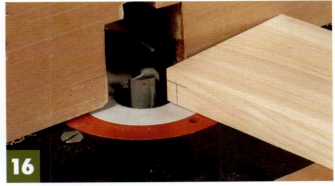

16 Make the buttons that will be used to fix the top in place. They are made from short lengths of board that are rabbeted on the end. Take a board and mark out the rabbet. The width should be ³⁄₁₆ in. (10 mm) and the protruding tongue on the end should be ¼ in. (6 mm) thick, to match the groove in the rails. Have a trial run and check the fit. If it is no good, you can always simply saw the tongue off the end and then reset the router and try again until you are happy with the fit.

17 After machining, cut the lumber to length—about 1 ⁹⁄₁₆ in. (40 mm). Cut the buttons to width—about ¾ in. (20 mm). The precise dimensions of the buttons are not critical, as long as they are large enough to locate in the groove and screw securely into the underside of the tabletop. Drill a clearance hole in each button, ³⁄₁₆ in. (4 mm) in diameter, and countersink for neatness.

18 Mark out the position of the frame on the underside of the top. Mark the position of the corners with a pencil.

19 ◀ Line up the frame with the pencil marks and screw the buttons into position. Put three along the short rails and two along the long ones. The buttons on the short rails may be pushed right into the bottom of the groove, but on the longer rails leave a little space, so that there is room for the top to expand to cope with changes in humidity.

20

21

Fit the router with the 1/16 in. (1.5 mm) straight cutter and place it on the tabletop. Adjust the side fence so that the cutter is exactly 2 15/16 in. (75 mm) from the table edge. To set the depth of cut accurately, carefully plunge the cutter, with the power switched off, until it just touches the surface. Lock the router down and take a short length of the inlay. Place it on top of the depth-setting turret and wind the depth adjuster down until the inlay is tightly sandwiched between the two. Lock the depth adjuster in place and remove the inlay. Now the router depth is set correctly.

Pull the router back to the corner mark and make sure that the cutter is just inside it. Keep the fence firmly against the edge, start the motor, and plunge the cutter. Slowly cut the groove along the table. Make sure that you stop before you get close to the end line. Repeat this on the other three sides and then reset the router fence to 2 in. (50 mm) from the side.

Inlays

Inlaying used to be a fairly demanding operation, but with a router, it becomes much easier. Inlaying involves cutting a groove in a surface and inserting a contrasting lumber or decorative line into it. This is then smoothed to match the surrounding surface. Inlay lines are available in a wide range of designs and sizes, and router cutters are made to match standard sizes.

This side table has an inlaid stained boxwood line, which really is not difficult to do. Begin by preparing the surface of the table: it must be properly sanded and smooth. Carefully mark out the position of the line. You do not need to mark all around. The most important points are the corners—it is vital not to rout your groove too long, otherwise the table will be ruined. Use a combination square with the length set at 2 in. (50 mm) to mark the corners.

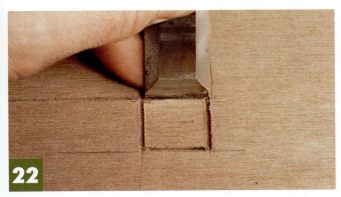

22 Cut the last two short sides of each corner. Again, be careful not to overshoot the marked line. The corner should now look something like this. The ends of the grooves will be left rounded by the router cutter. You need to square all these off with a chisel before the inlay can be fitted.

23 To make a neat corner joint, the ends of the inlay must be mitered. The simplest way to do this is to use a combination square and a chisel. Trap the inlay line under the square and make sure that it is hard against the reference fence. Place the flat side of the chisel against the rule and snip off the end of the inlay. As long as the chisel is sharp, this will produce the perfect miter.

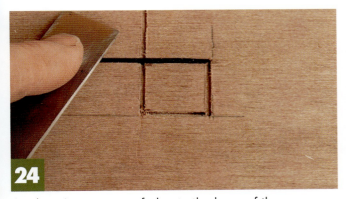

24 Apply a tiny amount of glue to the base of the groove using a sliver of wood or a pin. Press the inlay into place with the flat side of a chisel. Sometimes the groove and the inlay are not a perfect match, and the inlay will not fit. You need to sand the inlay's sides between your fingers to reduce the width.

25 Work slowly around the groove. Be patient and do not worry if you have cut a piece the wrong length, because you can always lever it out and replace it. The inlay should stand slightly proud of the surrounding surface.

◀ The inlay must be smoothed carefully. Do not use abrasive paper, as this will rub black dust from the line into the light wood surrounding it and turn the surface a muddy gray. Use a sharp chisel or a cabinet scraper and shave off the top until the surface is level and smooth.

26

Console Table

This project is fairly easy to undertake, but requires the ability to cut accurate 45-degree miters for fitting the legs to the rails. These are best cut on a table-mounted circular saw or a chop saw, but a manual miter saw will suffice as long as you mark the miter all the way around the lumber, clamp the wood to the saw bed, and take it slowly.

After cutting, the legs are smoothed with a spokeshave; a round-profile rasp will also do the job, but takes a little longer. A template of the leg design is shown on page 222, but you should experiment with alternative profiles. The only thing to remember is to minimize any short grain in the profile—this means any length of lumber that has been cut diagonally across the grain, leaving an area, usually a point, which can snap off if the grain at the point is short in length. The danger points are at the tip or toe of the leg and, for want of a better term, the ankle, so don't be too flamboyant in your design.

The finish on this table comes from a solution of instant coffee and water, which gives an attractive aged look, and then beeswax balsam rubbed over the surface.

Essential Tools & Materials

Tools

- pencil
- measuring tape
- combination square
- awl
- screwdriver
- hammer
- crosscut saw
- coping saw (or jigsaw with scrolling blade)
- power drill, ⅛ in. (3 mm) wood bit, countersink bit
- workbench
- belt sander (optional)

Hardware etc.

- 8 countersink screws 2 ¹⁵⁄₁₆ in. (75 mm) x No. 10
- 16 countersink screws 1⅜ in. (35 mm) x No. 8
- 40 countersink screws ¹¹⁄₁₆ in. (18 mm) x No. 6
- 8 shrinkage plates
- sandpaper in grits 80 to 150
- PVA wood glue
- approximately 30 molding pins ¾ in. (20 mm) long

Wood

- 90⁹⁄₁₆ x 7⅞ x 1 in. (2300 x 200 x 25 mm) pine or similar
- 141¾ x 4 x 1 in. (3600 x 100 x 25 mm) pine or similar
- 1⅜ in. x 4 x 1⅜ in. (3800 x 100 x 35 mm) pine or similar
- 126 x ¾ in. (3200 x 20 mm) hardwood decorative lipping

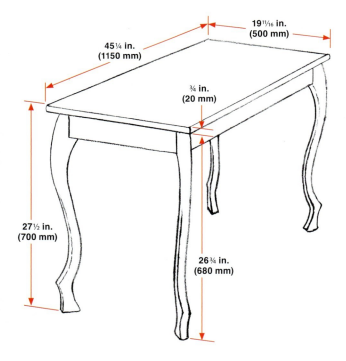

19¹¹⁄₁₆ in. (500 mm)

45¼ in. (1150 mm)

¾ in. (20 mm)

27½ in. (700 mm)

26¾ in. (680 mm)

Apart from the lipping around the edge of the tabletop, you can use ordinary lumber, carefully selected for lack of knots.

1 To start, you need to prepare the legs. Cut the 4 x 1⅜ in. (100 x 35 mm) section lumber into four equal lengths, and square each length across the ends. Measure up 36¾ in. (680 mm) and square another line around each leg. Take a tracing of the leg template on page 222, or make one of your own design, then lay it over one leg and press down the design through to the wood, reinforcing it with a pencil mark on the lumber as you go. Mark this leg as your pattern for shaping the other three.

2 Ensure that the leg is secured to your bench, and carefully cut out to the line with a jigsaw. Saw off the excess from the length and put aside. The scrap pieces from the legs will form the corner blocks that secure the legs of the table to the frame.

TIP

To avoid damaging the faces of the rails when you tighten up the clamps, saw off the sharp points from the small scrap blocks.

3 Shape the leg with a spokeshave, Surform tool, or rasp. When the cut is roughly square and you are happy with the basic shape, place it on the other three leg lengths, draw around it, and repeat steps 2 and 3. Finish all the legs with a belt sander or sandpaper until they are smooth and even. Do not sand the tops of the legs at this stage.

4 Here one of the scrap blocks is being cut on a table saw, with the guard removed for the sake of clarity. The short point measurement (see step 5) is the same as the width of the back of the leg. Take care when cutting the blocks because it is essential that they are true and square; save the small scrap pieces.

5 To measure the rails from the 4 x 1 in. (100 x 25 mm) lumber, take the "long points," the widest distance between two angled lines: looking down onto the wood edge, make two square lines across the edge at a given distance apart. Use the 45-degree shoulder of your combination square to make two more lines at 45 degrees running toward each other, from the same places as the two square lines. Cut two lengths mitered at 39⅝ in. (1000 mm) between the long points, and two at 15¾ in. (400 mm).

◄ Mark out the mitered ends of each rail by halving the width and carrying this mark over to the front and back faces. Then take a biscuit and find the optimum placing for the cut: it should be not too near the outside face, otherwise you will run the risk of the cutter splitting out—you should find that the best place is about one-third into the miter from the short point. Then draw a line along the mitered face and continue it onto the edges, so that you can align the registration marks on the footplate of the biscuit jointer. Clamp the rail in the vise as shown, set the jointer to the correct depth, align the registration marks by adjusting the jointer's fence, and cut the slots for the biscuits (practice on some scrap beforehand). Then mark out the legs by transferring the marks from the rails onto the sides of the legs. The important thing to achieve in all this is that the short point of your rails should abut the back of the legs exactly. This is a tricky operation, so you will need to take care when you are marking out the legs.

◄ Cut the 7⅞ in. (200 mm) plank into two lengths, each of 45¼ in. (1150 mm), and the remainder of the 4 x 1 in. (100 x 25 mm) plank to the same length. Place the best faces uppermost and arrange them as you think best, with the 4 in. (100 mm) between the 7⅞ in. (200 mm) planks. To minimize any warping or bowing, place the end grain of each plank in alternate directions and mark these with a face mark. The centerline of the end biscuits should be about 2 in. (50 mm) from the ends of the planks, with all the other biscuits about 5 15/16 in. (150 mm) apart. Clamp each board face-side uppermost to your bench, with a slight overhang along the edge. Set the jointer to cut along the center of the edge, and align the registration mark with your pencil lines. Check that the depth is set to size 20 and cut all the slots on the three boards. Insert the biscuits as shown, then glue and clamp the boards.

◄ When the top is completely dry, turn it over and plane off any irregularities. Now check that the ends are all flush; if not, cut them square with a circular or handsaw. Assemble the legs, rails, and blocks, remembering to place the biscuits in the slots as you go. You can see that small blocks have been used as packing for the clamp—these are the scrap pieces from the corner blocks. Drill out and countersink six holes for the screws. Drive the screws almost home, then check each corner for a square and tight fit. When you are satisfied that all the joints are good, disassemble the piece, glue up, clamp together, and drive home the screws. Clean off any excess adhesive with a damp cloth and check the frame once more to ensure that it is absolutely true and square.

◄ Place the edge lipping against the relevant edge and mark the short points. Cut the miters with a backsaw (tenon saw) in a miter block or with a miter saw, and fix the edge lipping to the top, using glue and molding pins. Clean up with a sharp chisel. When the assembly is completely dry, center it over the upside-down tabletop and attach with the corner plates, as shown. These have slots running in two directions to allow movement of the top in relation to the rails. Place your screws in the middle of these slots, and use only the slot that runs parallel to the width of the top to fit the screws.

Bookends

Woodworkers can be terrible hoarders, particularly when it comes to lumber, hanging on to the smallest scrap pieces just in case they come in handy later. Here is a project that is an ideal way to make good use of these pieces: a pair of bookends decorated with quadrants of contrasting lumber. Only a small amount of lumber is needed, and the design can easily be modified to suit what you have. Two router cutters are used and there is one joint to make. The bookends as depicted were constructed of scrap pieces of rosewood, American black walnut, and mahogany.

Essential Tools & Materials

Tools
- measuring and marking tools
- plane
- backsaw (tenon saw)
- compass
- jigsaw (optional)
- coping saw
- bar clamps
- router, router table, straight cutter $^{11}/_{16}$ in. (18 mm) in diameter (smaller will do), bearing-guided rounding-over cutter

Hardware etc.
- sandpaper
- glue

Wood
- 2 pieces 6 $^{11}/_{16}$ x 4¾ x $^{11}/_{16}$ in. (170 x 120 x 18 mm) tulipwood (base)
- 2 pieces 7⅝ x 4¾ x $^{11}/_{16}$ in. (194 x 120 x 18 mm) tulipwood (upright)
- 2 pieces with radius of 2¾ in. (70 mm) scrap wood
- 2 pieces with radius of 4 in. (100 mm) scrap wood
- 2 pieces with radius of 5⅛ in. (130 mm) scrap wood

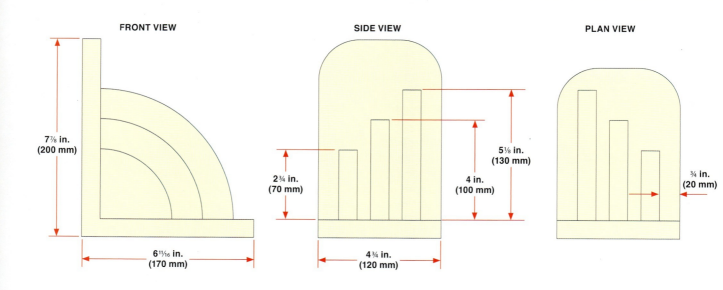

FRONT VIEW

7⅞ in. (200 mm)

6 $^{11}/_{16}$ in. (170 mm)

SIDE VIEW

2¾ in. (70 mm)

4¾ in. (120 mm)

PLAN VIEW

5⅛ in. (130 mm)

4 in. (100 mm)

¾ in. (20 mm)

Begin by preparing the lumber for the bases and the uprights. Make sure your lumber is an even thickness and that the sides are planed square and parallel. Mark out the dimensions and cut the boards to length with a backsaw (tenon saw).

The upright sits in a rabbet that is cut into the baseboard. The simplest way to mark this is by standing the upright in position on the baseboard with its edge flush with the end. Use a sharp pencil to mark the width of the rabbet on the base. Mark the depth of the rabbet—it should be about ½ in. (12 mm) deep.

The best way to cut a rabbet on a small board is to use the router table. Take a straight cutter and set it as shown. The fence is set so that the cutter just reaches the marked line for the width of the rabbet, and the height is set so that the cutter just reaches the marked line for the depth of the rabbet. Make several shallow passes until you reach the full depth. To avoid breakout, it is wise to run a backing board behind the workpiece.

Choose contrasting lumbers to make the quadrants. Mark out the lumber with a compass. The easiest way to make a quadrant is to cut out a half-circle and then divide it in half.

◄ A jigsaw is ideal for cutting out curved components such as these quadrants. However, a coping saw will do just as well. You could use the router and a jig or template to cut out the quadrants, but since there are so few to cut out, it would take more time than it is worth.

Once the quadrants have been cut out, smooth the edges with sandpaper. Fit a bearing-guided rounding-over cutter in the router table, and machine the curved edges of the quadrants on both sides. Bring the fence up so that it is in line with the bearing. Use it to lead the workpiece onto the cutter. (Grip the workpiece firmly so that there is no kickback on initial contact.) The rounding-over cutter does not make a deep cut, so the machining may be done in one pass, and the workpiece will be easy to control.

To soften the appearance of the bookends and echo the curves of the quadrants, round over the corners of the bases and the uprights. You can buy special templates of varying sizes to help you do this, but usually the easiest and cheapest way is to find some circular object, such as a can or jar lid, which provides the right sort of curve. Hold it over the corner of the workpiece, with its edges flush with the edges of the work, and draw around it with a pencil.

Cut off the corners with the jigsaw or coping saw, and then smooth the curve with a sanding block (a piece of scrap lumber with a piece of sandpaper wrapped around it). Now the main parts may be glued together. Apply a thin layer of glue to both surfaces of the rabbet. Position the upright in the rabbet and clamp the assembly together with a bar clamp. Make sure that the angle between the two components is 90°, otherwise it will be difficult to fit the quadrants. If you do not have a suitable clamp, a large rubber band could be used instead. Leave out to dry.

Remove the frames from their clamps once the glue has cured. Carefully sand the faces and edges and make sure that no traces of glue are visible. Soften all the edges with fine sandpaper. Position the quadrants and make sure that they will fit neatly. Place a piece of medium-grit sandpaper on the bench and smooth the flat edges of the quadrants to ensure a neat joint. Before gluing in the quadrants, make sure that the grain all runs in the same direction. Apply a thin layer of glue and carefully stick the quadrants in position.

Table Lamp

Good lighting is an essential part of any home and table lamps are a great way to light up the corners of a room. Here is an elegant design that makes the most of the router's decorative abilities. It takes the form of a square column with fluted faces. Both the base and the top are molded using a bearing-guided cutter. A light fitting is screwed to the top. Alternatively, a larger hole may be bored in the top and the same design used to make a candlestick.

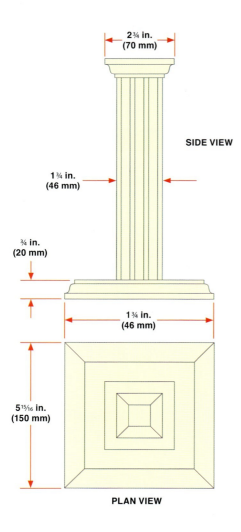

2¾ in.
(70 mm)

SIDE VIEW

1¾ in.
(46 mm)

¾ in.
(20 mm)

1¾ in.
(46 mm)

5¹⁵⁄₁₆ in.
(150 mm)

PLAN VIEW

Essential Tools & Materials

Tools
- measuring and marking tools
- G-clamps and spring clamps
- backsaw (tenon saw) or pullsaw
- drill
- jigsaw
- screwdriver
- router, router table, cove cutter: ⅜ in. (10 mm) in diameter, bearing-guided chamfer cutter, bearing-guided ogee cutter or similar

Hardware etc.
- sandpaper
- glue
- lamp fitting and cable to suit
- adhesive pads (optional)
- lampshade

Wood
- 2¾ x 2¾ x ¾ in. (70 x 70 x 20 mm) oak (top)
- 5¹⁵⁄₁₆ x 5¹⁵⁄₁₆ x ¾ in. (150 x 150 x 20 mm) oak (base)
- 37⁷⁄₁₆ x 1¹³⁄₁₆ x ½ in. (950 x 46 x 12 mm) oak (column sides)
- Eventual dimensions of each side are 8¼ x 1¹³⁄₁₆ x ½ in. (210 x 46 x 12 mm)
- 2 pieces 1 x 1 x 1 in. (25 x 25 x 25 mm) (mounting blocks)
- 9⅞ x 7⅞ in. (250 x 200 mm) scrap board (holding jig)

TIP

The column is made from four lengths of lumber with three flutes routed into them. The most difficult part of this project is getting the flutes evenly spaced. Experiment on a scrap piece until the spacing looks right. Remember that you only need to set the side fence twice, because both the outside flutes may be cut using the same setting, by reversing the workpiece.

Table Lamp

1 Using a ruler, square, and pencil, mark out the flute positions for the sides of the lamp on the single length of lumber for the column (there will be enough waste at the end to allow you to clamp it securely to the workbench).

2 Clamp the workpiece to the edge of the workbench, making sure that it overhangs slightly so that the side fence will not touch the bench itself.

3 Fit the cove cutter and make a series of short cuts, adjusting the settings until you are happy with the result. The flutes should be about ³⁄₁₆ in. (4 mm) deep and may be cut in one pass.

4 Having finalized the settings, you can now mold the sides. Do not cut the sides to length before molding them.

5 The sides will be joined using a miter joint—use a bearing-guided chamfer cutter for this. The angle of this cutter is 45°, so it will produce a perfect miter joint. When molding the edge of a narrow workpiece, it is preferable to use a router table for safety and accuracy. Set the cutter height so that there is about 1/32 in. (1 mm) of the workpiece running against the bearing.

6 Use a straightedge to set the router table fence exactly level with the bearing.

7 Mold both edges, making sure that the flutes are facing upward. Be careful to keep your hands well away from the cutter.

8 Now cut the sides to length. Use a try square and a pencil to square the end.

Carefully make the cut using a fine-toothed saw.

Miter joints can be difficult to glue, however, the fluting on these makes it fairly easy. Run a thin line of glue down one face of the joint and press the two halves together. Make sure that the joint lines up on both ends. Secure it using small sprung clamps or even clothes pegs (which should situate easily in the flutes). Alternatively, adhesive tape can be used.

All four sides can be glued at the same time. Make sure that the column is perfectly square and set it aside until the glue has cured. Cut the pieces for the top and the base to size and make sure they are square and that the edges are smooth. Fit the bearing-guided ogee cutter to the router table and mold the edges of the base. Start on the end-grain and work in a clockwise direction so that you finish on the side grain. This will ensure that you end up with no breakout on the corners.

12 Molding the top is a little more complicated. Because it is so small, it is not safe to mold it freehand. You need to make a simple holding jig from a piece of scrap board. Take the top and place it on the board so that its side is flush with the long side of the board. Draw around it with a pencil. Cut out the waste with the jigsaw.

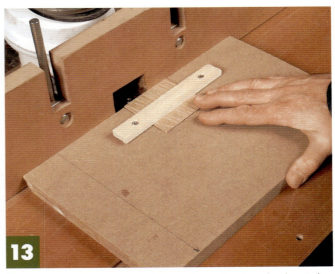

13 The top should slot snugly into the cutout in the board, and the edge must line up. Screw a thin lumber batten across the top to hold it down. Now start the router and run the whole board past the cutter. Take out the top, turn it around, and replace it. Repeat the process until all four sides have been molded.

14 To assemble the lamp, you first need to make up two small blocks with sides approximately 1 in. (25 mm) long. These should be adjusted so that they fit snugly into the ends of the column. Once you are happy with the fit, glue one block in the center of the base and the other onto the underside of the top. When the glue has cured, drill a hole (large enough to take the electric cable) through the center of both blocks.

15 You need to provide clearance for the cable under the base. This can be done either by using the cove cutter to make a straight cut from the center hole to the edge of the base, which is deep enough to contain the cable or, alternatively, you could stick adhesive pads on the underside of the base to raise it up and provide space that way. Before finally gluing the components together, install the cable and fit the light fitting. Refer to a qualified electrician if necessary.

Wastepaper Basket

A chic wastepaper basket makes all the difference to a room, whether it is an office or a living room. Here is a modern design that should be at home in almost any situation. With its elegantly sloping sides and contrasting wood types, it is almost too good to put trash in. The lumbers are sweet chestnut and American black walnut.

Essential Tools & Materials

Tools
- measuring and marking tools
- panel saw
- plane
- backsaw (tenon saw) or pullsaw
- bar clamp
- webbing clamp
- G-clamp
- screwdriver
- router, router table, straight cutter: 3/8 in. (10 mm), bearing-guided chamfer cutter

Hardware etc.
- sandpaper
- glue
- screws, 1/8 x 1/2 in. (3 x 13 mm)

Wood
- 4 pieces, 15¾ x 1³⁄₁₆ x ¾ in. (400 x 30 x 20 mm) American black walnut (corner posts)
- 4 pieces 9⅞ x 11 ¹³⁄₁₆ x ⅜ in. (250 x 300 x 10 mm) sweet chestnut (panels)

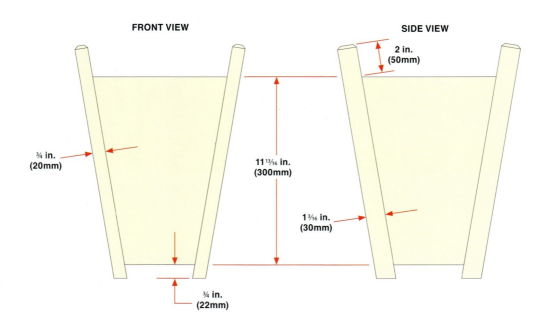

FRONT VIEW

SIDE VIEW

2 in. (50mm)

¾ in. (20mm)

11 ¹³⁄₁₆ in. (300mm)

1 ³⁄₁₆ in. (30mm)

¾ in. (22mm)

1

Start by marking out the side panels. To save material, the panels are arranged side by side with every alternate one inverted. The grain of the lumber should run across the panels. Leave a small space between them to allow space for the saw cut.

2

Carefully cut out the panels with the saw. Clean up the edges with a plane if necessary. Mark out the position of the panels on the corner posts. The corner posts should be cut to 15¾ in. (400 mm) in length. Mark the central point and then measure and mark a point 5¾ in. (145 mm) each side of this. The total length of the groove for the panel is 11⁷⁄₁₆ in. (290 mm). Carry these end marks around the posts.

3

Fit the straight cutter into the router table. Set the depth of cut to ¼ in. (6 mm). Using one of the corner posts, line up the cutter so that it is in the center of the face that is ¾ in. (20 mm) wide. This setting is not critical, but try to get it as near as possible.

4

As the groove is not going to run the full length of the post, you need to fit stop blocks to the router fence to prevent the marks being overrun. Place the post on top of the cutter, with the power off. Position it so that the front mark is just over the front tip of the cutter. Clamp a block onto the fence so that it is just in contact with the back end of the post. Tighten the clamp and check the setting. Now repeat the process with the back mark, and this time clamp a block onto the fence at the front end of the post.

5 To cut the grooves, care is needed. Start the router and place the post with its back end hard against the rear block, while holding the front end well above the cutter. Keeping it tight against the fence, lower the post onto the cutter and let it plunge in until the post is flat on the table. Then push the post forward until it contacts the front block. Carefully lift it off the cutter, keeping it tight against the fence. Repeat the process on the adjacent face and on the other three posts.

6 The groove is deliberately cut a little too short to accommodate the panel. This is to allow a small overlap on the panel at either end, to cover the end of the groove should any shrinkage occur. Therefore you need to cut a small notch on either end of the panels. To work out the size of the notch, push one panel into the groove and, using a sharp pencil, mark the depth on the panel. Take the panel out and put it beside the post. Mark the length of the groove on the panel, and then make a mark 3/16 in. (5 mm) or so back on either end.

7 Cut out the notches using a backsaw (tenon saw) or pullsaw. Assemble the basket without gluing to check for any problems.

8 The next job is to level the feet. While the basket is still assembled, stand it on a level surface and mark around each foot using a ruler. Make sure that the side of the ruler is flat against the bench.

◀ Dismantle the basket and carefully trim the ends of the feet to the marked lines. Sand the ends smooth.

9

10

The tops of the posts are chamfered on all four sides. End-grain molding is tricky to do so use a supporting board to stop the workpiece from slipping into the cutter. Fit the bearing-guided chamfer cutter into the router table and adjust the depth of cut. Align the fence with the guide bearing using a metal rule. Take a square-ended scrap piece and clamp it to the back of the post. Make sure that the ends of both pieces are exactly in line, and that the clamp is a safe distance from the cutter.

11

To make the cut, start the router and, holding the board and the post hard against the fence, run it past the cutter. Let the cutter mold the end of the post and cut into the supporting board. Remove the post from the board, turn it over, re-clamp, and repeat the process until all four edges are molded. Repeat on all the posts.

12

The posts are now finished, and the final job before assembly is to fit supporting blocks to hold the base panel. These are simply short lengths of lumber, ⅜ in. (10 mm) square, glued to the bottom inside edge of the panels.

13

Glue the posts onto two panels and let them dry, and then glue the other two panels in place. Do not use too much glue here, because the posts are fitted across the grain of the panels and must not restrict any movement. Only glue the center portion of the panel into the groove. Do not glue more than one-third of the panel length.

14

Clamping up a tapered assembly is awkward because the clamps will simply slide off. Here is a simple solution. First, clamp both assemblies together with a bar clamp to give two parallel sides for the clamp to work on. You will encounter another problem as you tighten the clamp—the two center posts will slide out of line. To stop this from happening, take a piece of folded sandpaper and sandwich it between the posts before applying the clamping pressure. This will stop them from moving.

15

You do not need to use great pressure to hold these panels together. Use a single bar clamp and tighten it just enough to push the panels fully into the grooves.

16

Once the glue has cured, the second pair of panels can be glued in place. Holding the assembly together is difficult—the solution is to use a webbing clamp or a roof rack strap. Wrap it around the center of the two previously glued panels to hold the other panels in position. Do not over-tighten.

17

Finally, make the base panel. This is made from a scrap piece of sweet chestnut, but you could easily use plywood. The tapered sides make it difficult to measure, and the corners have to be notched to suit the posts, so it is a good idea to make a cardboard template first.

18

Fix the base panel in position with a pair of screws through the supporting battens.

Shoe Rack

How do you store your shoes? Shoes tend to get scattered all around the house, strategically positioned to trip you. Here is a design for a proper shoe rack to keep them all tidied away. It is extremely simple to make, but also solid and reliable. Beech has been used for the sides and cherry for the rails, but you can use any lumber that you like, and a mix of lumbers can be attractive. The jointing is straightforward and a pocket hole jig is used to bore the ends of the support rails for easy attachment to the side panels.

Essential Tools & Materials

Tools

- measuring and marking tools
- backsaw (tenon saw)
- bench hook
- F- or G-clamp
- pocket hole jig
- plane
- sander
- drill and drill bit: $\frac{3}{16}$ in. (4 mm)
- screwdriver
- router, router table, bearing-guided chamfer cutter, straight cutter: $\frac{3}{4}$ in. (20 mm)

Hardware etc.

- sandpaper

Wood

- 2 pieces $15\frac{3}{4}$ x 11 $\frac{13}{16}$ x $\frac{3}{4}$ in. (400 x 300 x 20 mm) beech (sides)
- 2 pieces 27 $\frac{15}{16}$ x 1$\frac{3}{16}$ x $\frac{3}{4}$ in. (710 x 30 x 20 mm) cherry (rear rail)
- 4 pieces 26$\frac{3}{8}$ x 2 x $\frac{3}{4}$ in. (670 x 50 x 20 mm) cherry (support rail)

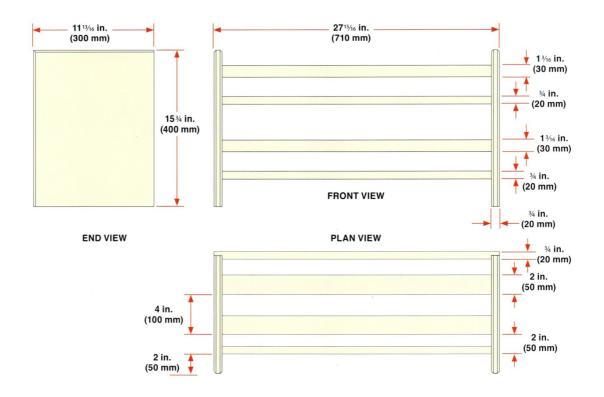

END VIEW

FRONT VIEW

PLAN VIEW

1 Start by cutting the side panels to size and make sure that the edges are square and true. Mark out and cut the rear rails exactly to length. Use a backsaw (tenon saw) and a bench hook for an accurate result.

2 Place the rails on the workbench and stand the side panel vertically across them, making sure that the ends are flush with the outside face of the side panel. Use a pencil to mark the width of the panel on the rail. You only need to do this on one rail end.

3 Take the combination square and mark a line along the center of the thickness of the rail. This is obviously ⅜ in. (10 mm) from the edge. This measurement is not critical—a millimeter or so either way will make little difference.

4 Fit the straight cutter to the router table. Put the marked rail on the table and raise the cutter up to the level of the marked centerline. Set the fence back so that the outer edge of the cutter just reaches the shoulder (vertical) line.

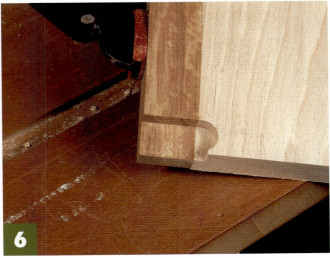

It is not safe to try to mold the end of a narrow rail without support. You can either use a sliding miter fence or, alternatively, a lumber support block. The support block can be any piece of reasonably wide scrap lumber. It must, however, have an accurately cut square end. Use a clamp to attach the rail to the front of it and make sure that the rail end and the block square end are absolutely level. Make the cut by running the block along, hard against the fence, and push the rail through the cutter. Let the cutter cut into the support board.

This is what the joint looks like after machining. The support board ensures that you get a clean cut without any breakout from the back of the rail.

Once you have machined the four ends of the rear rails, place one on the workbench and use it to mark the precise length of the supporting rails. These should be identical in length to the shoulder lines on the rear rails. Align the end of the supporting rail with the shoulder on the rear rail, and mark the other end with a square and a pencil.

Mark out the positions of all the supporting rails on the inside faces of the side panels. Use one of the rails to simplify the process.

9

For ease of assembly, the rails are screwed into the side panels from the inside. To do this accurately, you need to use a pocket hole jig. These are very simple to use and once set according to the manufacturer's instructions, it is just a matter of clamping each rail in the jig and drilling a pair of holes through the end. Make sure that you drill all the holes on the underside of the rails.

10

To add a little decoration to an otherwise rather stark structure, use the bearing-guided chamfer cutter to mold the edges of all the components. Fit the cutter to the router table and line up the fence with the roller bearing.

11

Mold both the upper edges of the support rails and the front upper and lower edges of the rear rails.

12

Mold the top and the front edges of the side panels. Mold the top edge first and finish on the front. Mold both the inside and outside faces.

Sand all the rails smooth and start to assemble the rack. Place a side panel on the workbench with its inside face upward. Clamp a batten across it along the line where the rails are to fit. This is to ensure that the rail doesn't move while the screws (which are set at an angle) are tightened. Place a rail in its marked position and screw it to the panel tightly.

Continue this process until all the rails are attached in place on both side panels.

Stand the rack on the workbench and fit both of the rear rails in place. Drill through the rail into the side panel and attach with one screw on each end.

Tray

This tray has endless uses—from breakfast in bed to drinks in the garden. It is simple to make and exploits the router's jointing capabilities. The frame and the base have been made from contrasting lumbers—American black walnut for the frame and chestnut for the base—but any lumbers may be used. Miter joints are used at the corners: these must be accurately cut, so you will need a sharp saw with a good miter guide. The final finishing is also important, because the tray will be handled a lot and so it must feel smooth and comfortable to hold.

Essential Tools & Materials

Tools
- measuring and marking tools
- try square
- jigsaw (optional)
- coping saw
- vise
- ripsaw
- crosscut saw with miter guide
- G-clamps
- band clamp or adhesive tape
- block plane
- router, router table, straight cutters: ¼ in. (6 mm) and ⅜ in. (9 or 10 mm), bearing-guided (or pin-guided) rounding-over cutter, slotting cutter: ³⁄₁₆ in. (4 mm), v-groove cutter

Hardware etc.
- sandpaper
- glue

Wood
- 2 pieces 23⅝ x 1⁹⁄₁₆ x ⅜ in. (600 x 40 x 9 mm) American black walnut (sides)
- 2 pieces 15 x 2¾ x ⅜ in. (380 x 70 x 9 mm) American black walnut (ends)
- 5 pieces 23⅝ x 3⁵⁄₁₆ x ⅜ in. (600 x 85 x 9 mm) chestnut (base)
- 1 piece 9⅞ x 2½ x ½ in. (250 x 60 x 12 mm) MDF (jig)

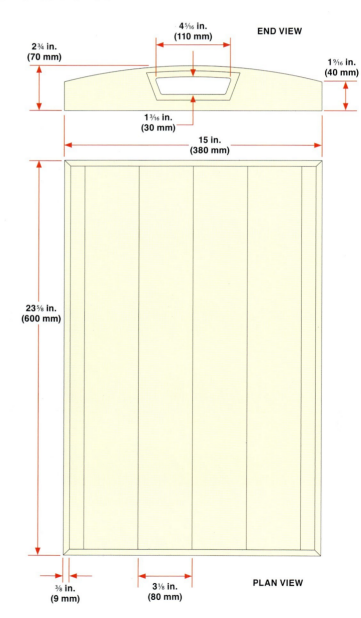

END VIEW

4⁵⁄₁₆ in. (110 mm)

2¾ in. (70 mm)

1⁹⁄₁₆ in. (40 mm)

1³⁄₁₆ in. (30 mm)

15 in. (380 mm)

23⅝ in. (600 mm)

⅜ in. (9 mm)

3⅛ in. (80 mm)

PLAN VIEW

1

Start by preparing the two ends of the frame. These are the most demanding parts to make, because you have to make the curves and the handles match. Mark out the lumber with the length of the component and then mark the height at the ends, 1 9/16 in. (40 mm), and the height at the center, 2 ¾ in. (70 mm). To produce a smooth curve through these three points, take a thin piece of lumber or plywood, and gently flex it with your hands at either end so that it bends evenly. Hold it over the workpiece so that it passes through the three points, and then get a helper to draw the curve on the lumber.

2

Cut out the curve using either a jigsaw or a coping saw, as shown here. Do not square the ends yet, but leave the piece overlong. Use it as a template to mark out the other end and cut it out as well. However well you manage to follow the marked line, there will still be some discrepancies between the two ends. Clamp them together in a vise and, using a sanding block, smooth the edges until they match. Prepare the two side pieces, but leave them a little overlong and also slightly wider by about 1/16 in. (2 mm). This will be planed off later.

3

The base of the tray is held in a groove that is routed into the inside faces of the sides and the ends. Choose a cutter to match the thickness of the baseboards, ideally about ⅜ in. (10 mm). Fit it into the router table and set the cutter height to 3/16 in. (4 mm) above the table. The distance from the fence should also be about 3/16 in. (4 mm). Make a test cut on a scrap piece to verify the settings. Then cut the groove on the inside face of all four components.

4

Now cut all four sides to length. The joint is a miter joint, and the easiest way to cut this is to use a dedicated miter saw. However, you can also use a backsaw (tenon saw) with a miter box. Again, if you are unsure about the accuracy of your saw, make a test cut using scrap pieces, so that you can then make adjustments if necessary.

5

◀ Make a handle jig (see Making a Handle Jig). Before making the cut, place the router on the jig with the power off, and move it around the recess to make sure that its path is clear and that the clamps do not get in the way. Ensure that the power cable is also safely positioned. To cut out the handle, place the router in the recess with the guidebush hard against the edge. Start the motor and plunge the cutter so that it just goes into the workpiece. Move the router smoothly around the jig in a clockwise direction until you have completed one circuit. Release the plunge lock and plunge the cutter a little further into the work, then repeat the circuit. Continue until you break through. Keep the router moving evenly so that you do not burn the lumber, and make several shallow passes.

Making A Handle Jig

The next job is to cut out the handle holes in each end. You could easily do this freehand with a coping saw or jigsaw; however, it really does look neater if both are identical. To ensure this, spend five minutes making a jig. For this job you need a straight cutter—¼ in. (6 mm) in diameter is ideal—and a guidebush fitted to the router base.

To make the jig, first draw round one of the ends on the piece of MDF. Then draw the position of the handle. Calculate the difference between the cutter and the guidebush in order to determine the template size. For example, if the guidebush is ¹⁵⁄₁₆ in. (24 mm) in diameter and the cutter is ¼ in. (6 mm) in diameter, halve the two sizes and subtract the smaller from the larger—the difference here is ⅜ in. (9 mm). So draw a line around the handle exactly ⅜ in. (9 mm) outside the existing line, and cut this out with a jigsaw. To help situate the end piece in the jig, pin three thin lumber strips on the MDF. The end piece will now fit precisely into the jig. Attach it in place with a couple of clamps at the ends.

Invert the jig with the end piece clamped in position, and attach the whole assembly to the edge of the bench so that it overhangs. Fit the router with the ¼ in. (6 mm) cutter and the guidebush.

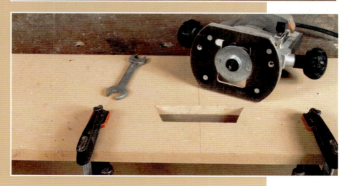

6

The handles must be comfortable to hold, so the lumber has to be smooth and rounded. Use a bearing- or pin-guided rounding-over cutter fitted in the router table to machine both sides of the handle. Because of the shape of the handle, the cutter will not be able to reach right into the corners, so you will have to finish these with a piece of sandpaper. The frame is now complete.

7

The boards for the base could simply be laid edge to edge in the frame, but a more attractive solution is to use tongue-and-groove joints. You can buy dedicated cutter sets to cut these joints, but they tend to be expensive and only suitable for a limited range of lumber thicknesses. I prefer to use a slotting cutter, which can be used to cut both parts of the joint, and then form the decorative chamfer using a V-groove cutter.

8

To cut the grooves you will need to work on the router table. Always cut the groove first, since it is much easier to make a tongue to fit a groove, rather than vice versa. Set the cutter in the table so that it lines up with the center of the board thickness. Adjust the fence so that the groove depth is ³⁄₁₆ in. (10 mm). Check the settings then cut a groove on one edge of each of the baseboards.

9

To cut the tongue, reset the cutter using the groove as a guide. Do not touch the fence setting, but simply lower the cutter in the table until its top edge lines up with bottom edge of the groove. This setting is a little fiddly to get right, so do experiment on scrap pieces first.

10

Cut the tongue in two passes by making one cut on one edge and then flipping over the board and making a second cut on the other edge. This ensures that the tongue is centrally positioned on the board.

11

To finish the baseboards, you need to put a small chamfer on either side of the joint. The reason for this is to make a feature of the joint rather than try to conceal it. It also has the effect of making it more difficult to see if there is any discrepancy between the gaps of the individual joints. Use the V-groove cutter and set it as shown. Make sure that it does not cut into the tongue. Reset the fence and do the same to the grooved edge.

A section through the board after the routing has been completed

Trim and arrange the boards ready for assembly. Crosscut them to length first and then set them out with four full-width boards across the center and two narrow boards on either side. The two side boards will need to be ripped to width. Make sure that you do this evenly, so that the boards are centralized across the tray. When all the boards are joined together, they should be a slightly loose fit across the tray to allow for any expansion.

To strengthen the tray frame, you can glue both the outside boards into the side grooves.

Now assemble all the parts. Apply a little glue to each of the corner joints and the ends of the outer boards. Make sure that no glue gets into the end grooves or onto any of the other baseboards.

Clamp the tray using a band clamp. Once the glue has cured, remove the clamp and clean up the edges. The sides need to be planed down to match the angle of the end pieces. Do this with a block plane, working from both ends. Finally, go over the whole piece with sandpaper.

Paneled Coffee Table

Living rooms are not as large as they used to be, so any furniture needs to earn its keep. This design for a small coffee table also features convenient and unusual storage space: the top panels slide open to give access to the space below. The panels are made from a contrasting lumber and slide in grooves cut into the top boards. Beech has been used for the frame and American cherry for the sliding panels.

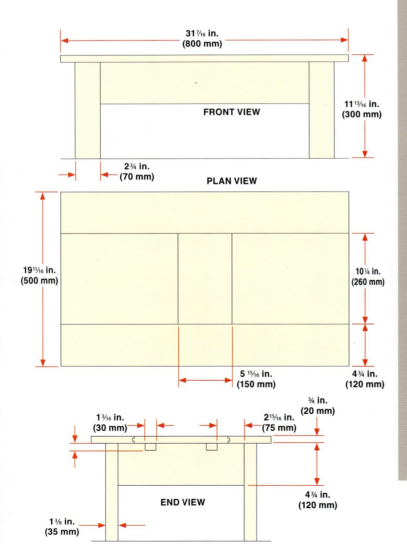

FRONT VIEW

31 7/16 in. (800 mm)

11 13/16 in. (300 mm)

2 3/4 in. (70 mm)

PLAN VIEW

19 11/16 in. (500 mm)

10 1/4 in. (260 mm)

5 15/16 in. (150 mm)

4 3/4 in. (120 mm)

END VIEW

1 3/16 in. (30 mm)

2 15/16 in. (75 mm)

3/4 in. (20 mm)

4 3/4 in. (120 mm)

1 3/8 in. (35 mm)

Essential Tools & Materials

Tools
- measuring and marking tools
- F- or G-clamp
- backsaw (tenon saw)
- ripsaw
- coping saw
- jigsaw (optional)
- plane and orbital sander
- bar clamps
- biscuit jointer
- pocket hole jig
- screwdriver
- chisels
- router, router table, slotting cutter: 3/16 in. (4 mm), straight cutters: 3/8 in. (9 mm) and 11/16 in. (18 mm)

Hardware etc.
- glue
- sandpaper
- screws: 16 x 3/16 x 1 in. (4 x 25 mm)

Wood
- 4 pieces 11 x 2 15/16 x 1 3/8 in. (280 x 70 x 35 mm) beech (legs)
- 2 pieces 24 3/8 x 4 3/4 x 3/4 in. (620 x 120 x 20 mm) beech (side rails)
- 2 pieces 15 3/8 x 4 3/4 x 3/4 in. (390 x 120 x 20 mm) beech (end rails)
- 10 13/16 x 5 5/16 x 3/4 in. (275 x 150 x 20 mm) beech (center rail)
- 2 pieces 31 7/16 x 4 3/4 x 3/4 in. (800 x 120 x 20 mm) beech (top)
- 10 13/16 x 5 5/16 x 3/4 in. (275 x 150 x 20 mm) beech (center)
- 2 pieces 11 x 14 3/16 x 3/4 in. (280 x 360 x 20 mm) cherry (sliding panels)
- 26 3/4 x 15 x 1/4 in. (680 x 380 x 6 mm) MDF (base panel)

Cut the frame components to size (four legs, two side rails, and two end rails). The mortises must then be marked out. Lay one rail on top of a leg, making sure that the top of the leg is flush with the top of the board. Check that it is square and then mark the width of the rail on the leg. Extend the line onto the edge of the leg. Stand the leg on its edge and find the centerline. Mark this and then mark another horizontal line ⅜ in. (10 mm) down from the top. The mortise will be cut directly on the centerline and between the two marked horizontal lines.

One difficulty with cutting mortises near to the end of components is that there is little support for the router and so it can topple off. The simplest way to prevent this is to clamp two legs end to end on the bench, and then cut the joints so that as the router runs off the top of one leg it is still supported by the end of the other leg.

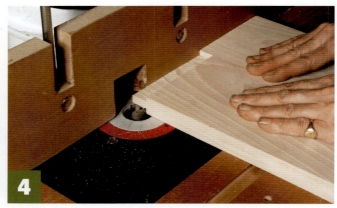

Cut the joint: line up the cutter on the centerline and lock the side fence. Use the ⅜ in. (9 mm) cutter and set the depth of cut to just over ¾ in. (20 mm). Cut the joint in a series of passes, making sure that you do not go over the horizontal lines. Repeat this on both faces of each leg, using the same fence setting (so that both mortises are the same distance from the outside edge). The router will obviously cut a round-ended mortise. You can either make a round-ended tenon to fit it or square off the ends of the mortise with a chisel.

The tenons are cut on the router table. Mark the length of the tenon, ¾ in. (20 mm), on the end of the rail. Fit the larger straight cutter into the router table. Now set the fence so that the cutter will just reach the marked line. To achieve the correct tenon thickness, make a shallow pass on each side and then check the fit in the mortise. Repeat the process, making passes equally on both sides until the tenon is a snug fit in the mortise. At this stage it will be too long. Trim off the top ⅜ in. (10 mm) of the tenon with a tenon saw to match the mortise.

Because the frame of the table also provides the storage space, a bottom panel will be fitted once the rest of the table is complete. However, you need to cut the rabbet for it before the frame is assembled. Again, do this on the router table using a straight cutter. Set the height of the cutter so that it reaches about halfway into the thickness of the side rail, and fence so that the width of the rabbet is about ¼ in. (7 mm). Machine all four sides of the completed rabbet.

The sliding panels will have supporting bars fixed to their underside to hold them flat. The end rails must have cutouts to accommodate these. Refer to the drawing, mark out, and make a series of vertical saw cuts using a backsaw (tenon saw) or pullsaw. Remove the waste with a coping saw and then clean up the base of the recess with a chisel.

Before assembling the frame, sand all the components with an orbital sander. Glue the frame together in two stages. First take the long rails and glue the legs onto each end. Apply glue to the mortise rather than the tenon, since it will then be pushed into the joint when the tenon is inserted. Use a bar clamp to hold the assembly together tightly while the glue cures.

Next, glue the shorter rails in place. Again, use the bar clamps and make sure that the whole frame is exactly square by measuring the diagonals with a rule. They must be identical. If they are not, remove the clamps and straighten the frame before reapplying the clamps. Make sure that the frame is standing on a perfectly level surface and that all the legs are stable.

Fit the central rail when the frame is complete. Measure the frame and cut the rail so that it is a sliding fit in the frame. To hold it in position, use a pocket hole jig and bore through both ends. Before installing the rail, use the pocket hole jig to make a series of holes along the top edge in order to attach the top down. Do the same on the main frame side rails.

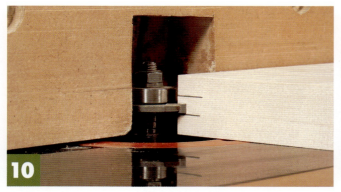

Make up the top boards. Start by preparing the two side boards. Cut the boards to length and set up the router table to machine the groove that the panels will slide along. It should be ⁵⁄₁₆ in. (8 mm) wide and ⅜ in. (10 mm) deep. Use a ³⁄₁₆ in. (4 mm) slotting cutter and make two passes, turning the board over in between. This ensures that the groove will be centrally positioned in the thickness of the board.

When you have completed the groove, place the boards in position on the frame and measure the precise length of the central board. You must measure into the bottom of the groove. Cut the board to this length and then groove the sides to match the side boards.

Now cut a matching tenon on both ends of the central board. Using an ¹¹⁄₁₆ in. (18 mm) straight cutter, make a shallow pass on each side of the board and then check the fit in the groove. Repeat this until the tenon is a snug fit in the groove.

Fix the jointed boards to the frame. It is important that the outside boards are exactly parallel, otherwise the sliding panels will not move smoothly. Position the boards on the frame—use a dab of glue in the center of the tenon on the center board, but do not glue its full width because it needs to be free to move. Clamp the boards in place, turn the table over, and screw through the pocket holes.

◀ To make up the sliding panels, you will need to joint together several boards edge to edge. When the panels are installed, the grain must run parallel to the center board, otherwise there is a risk of them expanding and jamming in their grooves. The boards must be prepared to the same thickness as the rest of the top. Strengthen the joints with a biscuit jointer.

15

The panels must be a precise fit in the grooves, so measure carefully before cutting them to size. Cut the tongues on three sides of the panels using the same technique as for making the tenons on the center board. Keep checking the fit after each pass, and make sure that you do not make them too thin. The panel should move smoothly within the groove, with an even gap on all sides. When satisfied with the fit, trim to length.

16

Because the width of the sliding panels is unsupported, they need to have bearer bars fixed to their undersides to hold them flat. These are attached with three screws each. The central screw is bored and countersunk as normal; however, the outer two holes must be enlarged along the length of the bearer to allow for any movement in the boards. Screw the bearers in place with the panels in position, and make sure that they line up with the cutouts in the end rails.

17

Finally, take a short scrap piece and attach it to the end of each panel to stop it from falling out of the table each time the panels are opened.

18

Once the panels have been fitted and are operating smoothly, the base panel can be fitted. Measure the rabbet and cut the panel to size. A backsaw (tenon saw) can be used to remove the corners to accommodate the legs. Screw the panel in place, so that it can be removed should there be any problems with the panels in the future.

Modernist Coffee Table

This table is very much a modernist design, with the only decoration being in the materials. Note that the tapered legs have a line in the grain that runs through all four legs and is ranged in the same direction. It is this attention to detail that can enhance your own furniture. The proportions are of paramount importance here, and the design will not respond well to adaptation unless the whole balance is reworked.

The board material is maple-veneered MDF, with edging strip ironed on to the exposed edges. The legs are solid lumber, biscuit-jointed to the underside of the table, and the boards are also biscuit-jointed.

Finish the table with clear varnish or cellulose because the surface will need a good protection, especially on the edges.

Essential Tools & Materials

Tools

- pencil
- measuring tape
- square
- marking knife
- ruler
- circular saw (table-mounted optional)
- orbital (palm) sander (optional)
- electric planer
- biscuit jointer and 38 size 20 biscuits
- ½ in. (12 mm) bevel-edge chisel
- jack plane
- block plane
- cabinet scraper, domestic iron, Workmate or workbench, G-clamps

Hardware etc.

- sandpaper in grits 150, 180, 280, 320, and 400
- two-part epoxy wood glue

Wood

- 2 pieces 46 x 17½ x ¾ in. (1170 x 445 x 20 mm) maple-veneered MDF
- 3 pieces 4⁵⁄₁₆ x 17½ x ¾ in. (110 x 445 x 20 mm) maple-veneered MDF
- 4 pieces 9¹⁄₁₆ x 2¹⁵⁄₁₆ x 2¹⁵⁄₁₆ in. (230 x 75 x 75 mm) maple
- 32 ft. (10 m) maple iron-on edging strip

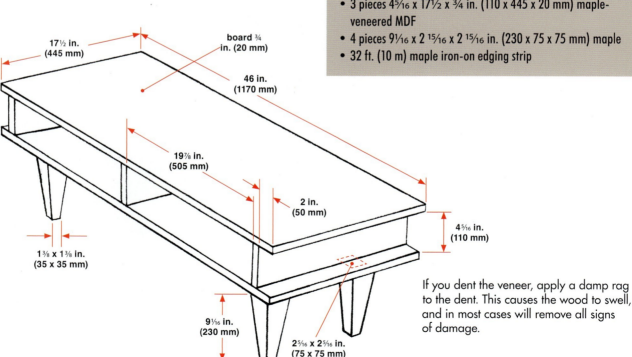

17½ in. (445 mm)

board ¾ in. (20 mm)

46 in. (1170 mm)

19⅞ in. (505 mm)

2 in. (50 mm)

4⁵⁄₁₆ in. (110 mm)

1⅜ x 1⅜ in. (35 x 35 mm)

9¹⁄₁₆ in. (230 mm)

2⁵⁄₁₆ x 2⁵⁄₁₆ in. (75 x 75 mm)

If you dent the veneer, apply a damp rag to the dent. This causes the wood to swell, and in most cases will remove all signs of damage.

1 Mark out the boards, using a knife to cut through the veneer; make two cuts for each saw cut separated by the width of the kerf, to avoid splitting the veneer. Lay the uprights across the bottom shelf, clamped as shown. Cut the slots for the bottom shelf, and repeat the process for the top.

2 When preparing the maple for the legs, you need four lengths cut exactly to 9 1/16 in. (230 mm). Mark the lengths with a knife and cut the barest distance from each knife cut, then use a sharp block plane to get the tops and bottoms perfectly flat and square. As you plane, you will begin to see the knife cuts appear on the surface; don't plane below them.

3 Mark each leg with a centerline marked on all four faces and both ends. The taper runs from the full width of 2 15/16 in. (75 mm) down to 1 3/8 in. (35 mm). Mark out the positions of the legs, 2 in. (50 mm) in from the front and back edges and 2 3/4 in. (70 mm) in from the ends on the underside of the table base.

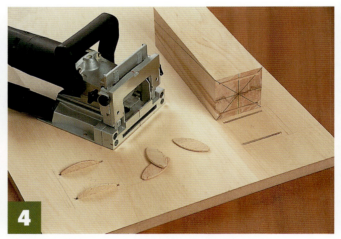

4 Clamp each leg up to the inner mark, ensuring that it is parallel to the edge of the base. Set the jointer plate to size 20 and cut the inner slot in both the leg and base as shown. Turn the leg around and repeat for the outer side. Repeat for each leg.

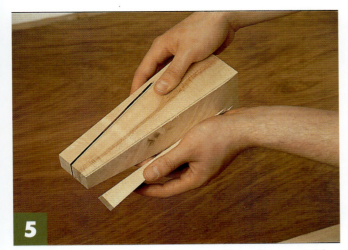

Remove the legs and cut the waste. If you have a table saw with a 2 15/16 in. (75 mm) or better depth of cut, this is a straightforward operation; however, you may have to remove the waste by plane or even by two passes through a smaller saw. Bring the legs to a smooth finish with a plane, and then finally use a cabinet scraper. Use the scrap pieces to hold the legs in the vise.

To apply the iron-on strip to the edges, set the iron to medium and apply firm pressure, checking that the glue has melted before moving on. Use a block plane to remove the excess edging strip.

Use an orbital (palm) sander to finish prior to assembly. Glue the top first: place three bearers over the uprights top and bottom, then clamp the ends of the bearers. When gluing the legs, the weight of the table is sufficient to dispense with clamps.

Projects for the Kitchen

144 Mug Shelf

150 Knife Block

162 Traditional Cupboard

172 Modernist Cupboard

158 Cutting Board

160 Knife Rack

176 Picture Rail Shelf

180 Kitchen Sink Makeover

Mug Shelf

In the kitchen, it is always a great idea to have the items you use most within easy reach. This simple set of shelves works wonderfully as a mug shelf but could easily be used for spice jars. Each shelf has a high front edge to keep everything securely in place and underneath there is a handy rail for hand towels. The shelves are traditionally jointed with housing joints, so the router cutter and lumber must be the same thickness. The lumbers used are ash and rosewood.

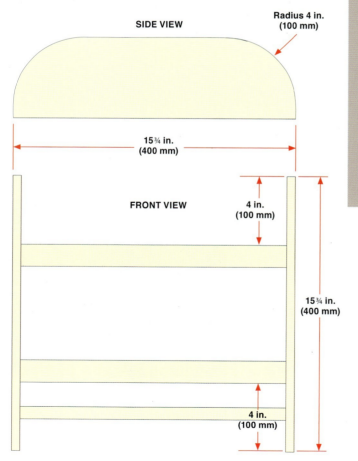

SIDE VIEW

Radius 4 in. (100 mm)

15¾ in. (400 mm)

FRONT VIEW

4 in. (100 mm)

15¾ in. (400 mm)

4 in. (100 mm)

1

Start by cutting the main components to length. Make sure that the ends are square and the sides are parallel. Line up the two side boards and mark out the position of the housings where the shelves will join.

2

Because the sides are wider than the shelves, the housings do not run their full width. Lay a shelf on top of the side, with the two back edges lined up. Mark the width of the shelf on the side. This marks the end of the housing.

3

The housings are routed out using a straight cutter of exactly the same thickness as the shelves, in this case ½ in. (12.7 mm). Set the depth of cut to ¼ in. (6 mm). You can cut the joints in both sides at the same time. Line up the boards, back to back, and make sure that the ends are perfectly level. Clamp a guide batten across the two boards with the G-clamps to guide the cutter exactly along the marked line. To make the cut, work from the right-hand side to the left—the cutter spins clockwise so it will keep pushing the router against the guide batten. If you move the router in the other direction, the cutter will be trying to pull the machine away from the batten all the time, and you will risk making an inaccurate cut.

4

After routing, the ends of the housings will be rounded. Square them off with a chisel.

5

To cut the curves on the ends of the side panels, use a trammel attachment on the router. This is simply a point that attaches to one of the fence rods, and around which the machine may be pivoted. Fit the router with a fairly small straight cutter of around ¼ in. (6 mm) in diameter. Use a steel ruler to set the radius to 4 in. (100 mm).

Place the side panel on the workbench on top of a piece of scrap lumber or sheet material. Mark a line ¾ in. (20 mm) in from the back edge and around 4 in. (100 mm) from the end. Clamp the panel to the workbench with the G-clamp.

Place the router on the workpiece and position the trammel point on the marked line. Lower the cutter to touch the surface and adjust the position of the machine so that the inside edge of the cutter just overhangs the end of the board. Swing the router around the trammel point and ensure that the cutter will exit smoothly from the front edge of the board. Once you are happy with the settings, you can make the cut.

Make several shallow passes until you finally cut into the scrap board below. Be sure to keep the pressure on the inside edge of the router to keep the trammel point firmly in the lumber.

A piece of hardwood dowel is used for the rail. The router can be used to bore the hole for this. Fit a straight ¹¹⁄₁₆ in. (18 mm) cutter and mark the position of the rail on the side panels with a cross. It should be set 2 in. (50 mm) in from the back and 2 in. (50 mm) up from the bottom edge. Set the depth of cut to ¼ in. (6 mm). The router will cut a very neat hole, but it can be difficult to hold it still while making the cut so use the side fence coupled with a G-clamp. Set the side fence to position the center of the cutter exactly 2 in. (50 mm) in. Clamp the board to the workbench, and put the router in position over the mark. Use a small G-clamp to hold the router securely in place. Depending on the design of the router and side fence, it may be tricky to get the clamp in place. You may find it easier to let the board overhang the side of the workbench a little. ▶

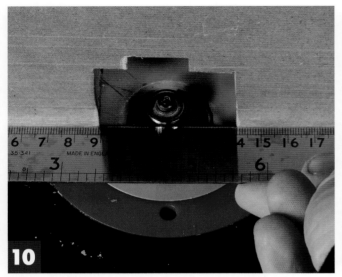

10 The next job is to round over the sides and the shelf fronts. Fit the router table with the bearing-guided rounding-over cutter and set the fence level with the bearing. Raise the cutter so that it will create a good radius.

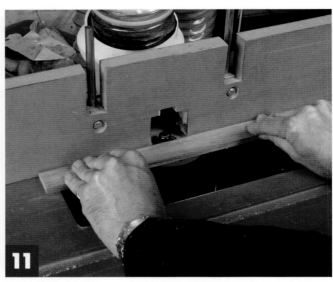

11 Cut the shelf fronts roughly to length and round over the top edges on both the inside and outside faces.

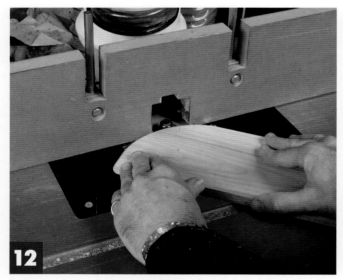

12 Round over both the side boards on the inside and outside faces. Be careful when routing the curved sections, because the end-grain will scorch if you move too slowly.

13 Before fitting the shelf fronts, it is worth cutting a shallow rabbet on the backs of them. Use the ½ in. (12.7 mm) straight cutter (or a larger one) in the router table, and use a scrap piece from the end of one of the shelves to set the width of the rabbet. Hold the scrap piece above the cutter and push the fence back until the front of the cutter is just flush with the front face of the scrap piece. Lock the fence in position and set the cutter about ³⁄₁₆ in. (4 mm) above the table. Carefully cut the rabbet on the inside of both the shelf fronts.

14

Assemble the shelves and measure the exact length of the shelf fronts, then cut the fronts to length with a backsaw (tenon saw) or pullsaw.

15

Apply glue to the housings and the holes for the rail. Assemble the shelves and clamp up with a pair of bar clamps in line with the shelves. Measure across the diagonals of the assembly to ensure that it is square. Both diagonals should be of equal length. If they do not match, loosen the clamps and realign the shelves before tightening the clamps again.

16

Once the main assembly is dry, the shelf fronts can be glued in place. Use a pair of clamps on each shelf to hold it in place until the glue dries. Finally, sand all surfaces and apply a finish. To attach the shelves to a wall, use a pair of metal mounting brackets, available from most hardware stores.

Knife Block

Kitchen knives need to be easily accessible, and it is important to store them safely. A knife block is a great solution. You can design one to hold all your knives and keep them sharp and ready for use. Here is a simple design that you can customize to suit your needs. It has been made in American black walnut and American white ash, but you can use any hardwood waste pieces that are lying around the workshop.

Essential Tools & Materials

Tools
- measuring and marking tools
- crosscut saw and ripsaw
- bar clamps
- mallet
- sander
- chisel
- plane
- G-clamp
- band clamp
- router, side fence, straight cutter: ¾ in. (19 mm), bearing-guided rounding-over cutter

Hardware etc.
- glue
- sandpaper
- oil to finish
- adhesive rubber feet

Wood
- 24 lengths (in total) of American black walnut and American white ash, 11 ¹³⁄₁₆ x ¾ x ¾ in. (300 x 20 x 20 mm)

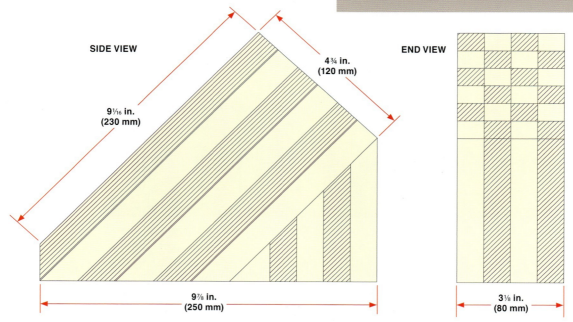

SIDE VIEW

4¾ in. (120 mm)

9¹⁄₁₆ in. (230 mm)

9⅞ in. (250 mm)

END VIEW

3⅛ in. (80 mm)

1 Prepare all the lumber. All the pieces should be the same length and thickness. They will be glued together to make four panels of six pieces.

2 Spread glue evenly on each piece and clamp the assembly tightly in a pair of bar clamps.

3 If you have a large pair of clamps, you can clamp up all four panels at the same time. Try to make sure that each piece is level and in line with the next. As you tighten the clamps, the pieces are inclined to slip a little, so re-check and tap into place with a mallet if necessary. Once the glue has set, remove the panels from the clamps and clean up with a sander until the surface is smooth. If there are any large lumps of dried glue, clean them off first with a chisel.

4 Once the boards are smooth, decide how to arrange your knives in the block. Stand the boards on their ends and sandwich the knives between them. Mark their position on the ends of the boards.

5

Lay the boards flat on the bench and mark out the width of each blade on the inside. Make sure that you leave enough space for curved blades, because otherwise the knife handle will not sit squarely in the block when the knife is inserted.

6

Use the knife blade itself to set the depth of cut on the router. Insert the cutter and plunge the router down, with the power off, so that the cutter is just touching the workpiece. Sandwich the knife blade in the depth adjuster as shown in the picture, then open it another millimeter or so to make it easy to insert and remove the knife.

7

One difficulty with routing boards of this length is that there is little space for the clamps. If you are careful, you can simply use one clamp. Start by clamping the board on the far end. Make sure that the edge of the board overhangs the bench edge.

8

Start routing the groove until the router contacts the clamp. Stop and reposition the clamp on the front end of the board and finish the cut. If the groove needs to be wider than the cutter width, reset the side fence and repeat the process.

9

◄ When all the grooves have been routed, glue all the boards together. Spread the glue evenly on each board.

10

Clamp up all the boards tightly. Use as many bar clamps as you can to ensure a really good bond.

11

Once the glue has cured, remove the bar clamps and clean up the sides with the sander. Lay the longest knife on the block to determine the length it needs to be. Use a combination square to mark a 45° cut on the base of the block. Extend the line around the edges of the block.

12

Cut off the end of the block as cleanly as possible using a backsaw (tenon saw).

13

Do not discard the scrap piece because it will be used to give added support to the block. Plane and sand the cut end so that it will join neatly onto the main piece. Trim it to fit.

Liberally coat the support piece with glue. End grain is very absorbent and this will not be an enormously strong joint (it does not actually need to be).

Because the block is an irregular shape, this is a slightly difficult joint to clamp up. The easiest method to use is a band clamp. Alternatively, a webbing roofrack strap with a ratchet buckle can be used.

Smooth the base of the knife block with a sander. Make sure that it is completely level so that the block will stand on a flat surface without rocking or wobbling.

Finally, you need to treat all the sharp edges. Fit the bearing-guided rounding-over cutter to the router and mold all the edges. Clamp the block to the workbench and work around the block, moving the clamp as necessary. To protect the base of the block from any kitchen worktop spills, attach a set of four adhesive rubber feet to support it.

Kitchen Accessories

Hardwood waste pieces should never be discarded in any workshop. It's a saying among lumberyard owners, that there's no such thing as scrap hardwood. Here are two projects that use scrap pieces. In both, the dimensions are to some degree flexible, depending on what you have at hand.

The cutting board is designed to be a mini version of a butcher's block, with end grain uppermost. Every block within the outer frame is a regular cross section cut from various odd lengths. If you wish to follow the herringbone arrangement illustrated, this regularity is essential. However, you can create a pattern of random widths all glued up together. The frame is dovetailed together using a single pin with an angle of 1:8. This is a simple joint, but requires a fair degree of accuracy and concentration. For the knife rack (shown on page 160), I used two contrasting lumbers separated by ¼ in. (6 mm) plywood fillets. I finished the chopping board with olive oil (you could use any vegetable oil), and the knife rack with Danish oil.

Essential Tools & Materials

Tools
- pencil
- measuring tape
- square
- sliding bevel
- backsaw (tenon saw) or dovetail saw
- crosscut saw
- bevel-edge chisel
- coping saw or jigsaw
- drill, ³⁄₁₆ in. (4 mm) wood bit, countersink bit
- jack plane
- block plane
- cabinet scraper
- Flexicurve or French curves
- workbench
- G-clamps
- table-mounted circular saw (optional)
- belt sander (optional)
- electric hand plane (optional)

Cutting Board

Hardware etc.
- two-part epoxy resin

Wood
- 2 pieces 14³⁄₁₆ x 1¾ x 1³⁄₁₆ in. (360 x 45 x 30 mm) maple
- 2 pieces 11 ¹³⁄₁₆ x 1¾ x 1³⁄₁₆ in. (300 x 45 x 30 mm) maple
- 95 pieces 1⅞ x 1¾ x ¾ in. (47 x 45 x 20 mm) ash

Knife Rack

Hardware etc.
- waterproof or water-resistant wood glue

Cutting Board

1

2

Collect short lengths of lumber of the same section, about 1 ¾ x ¾ in. (45 x 20 mm); you will need about 14 ft. 9 in.–16 ft. 5 in. (4.5–5 m) in total. Saw these accurately to 1 ⅞ in. (47 mm), ensuring that there are no defects near either end. Arrange them in rows of 12 in a herringbone pattern to create the main block. Cut two lengths of softwood batten 5 ¹⁵⁄₁₆ in. (150 mm) longer than the length of your assembled block and two lengths about ⅜ in. (10 mm) less than the width of the block.

Arrange the blocks, battens, and clamps as shown, then lay a sheet of newspaper over your bench and quickly apply some epoxy glue to all four faces of each block. Place the battens and clamps in place and tighten. If any outer block tends to pull away from the main body, adjust the position or tightness of the nearest clamp head, or force a small wedge of lumber into the side of the batten to correct the error. Scrape off any excess glue and clean up. When the glue has dried, plane one face flat and mark a square area, using the maximum amount of the block; it may be a good idea to allow a ¹⁄₁₆ in. (2 mm) margin of error in from the extreme edge of the block because it's far easier to plane the edge of the block than have to recut dovetail shoulders. This marked area will be the inside dimension of your frame. Prepare the frame parts and transfer the marks from the block to give the shoulders of the dovetails.

3 Mark out for the dovetails: square the shoulder marks around, then square around a second line the thickness of the lumbers (1 ¾₁₆ in. [30 mm]) out from the shoulder line. You will have some excess length, called "horns." Set a sliding bevel to a 1:8 slope—measure a line 3 ⅛ in. (80 mm) long on scrap wood, then mark a second line running square to the first ⅜ in. (10 mm) long and join the two lines with a diagonal to give a 1 in 8 bevel. For the pins, set a marking gauge to ⅜ in. (10 mm) and mark a point in from the edge on the second line drawn. Repeat at both ends, front and back, and on both short lengths.

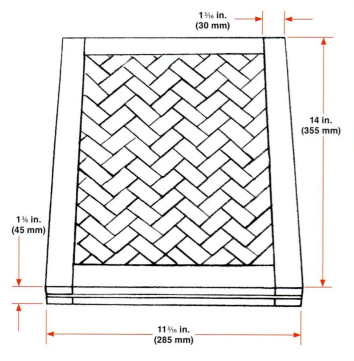

1 ³⁄₁₆ in. (30 mm)

14 in. (355 mm)

1 ¾ in. (45 mm)

11 ³⁄₁₆ in. (285 mm)

5 Mark out the sockets in the same fashion on the longer lengths: the stock of the sliding bevel will lie against the narrow edge as before, but this time the blade runs across the end grain. Use the marking gauge at ⅜ in. (10 mm) to run from the end grain down to the shoulder line, and reset it to the thickness of the narrowest width of the peg, about ¹¹⁄₁₆ in. (17 mm). Run this line down to the shoulder. Prior to cutting the sockets, lay all four lengths out on the bench and check that you have marked them correctly.

4 Use the sliding bevel with the stock against the narrow face to draw a line intersecting the ⅜ in. (10 mm) point down to the shoulder line. Repeat back and front and both ends. Join the bevels across the end grain and mount the lumber vertically in a vise. Saw just to the outside of your bevel lines, keeping the saw level. As you approach the shoulder line, check the back to ensure that you don't cut too deep. Turn the work to a horizontal position and cut to the shoulder line, just leaving the line in place.

TIP

Coping saws are difficult to control, owing to the narrowness of the blade, so check the cut continuously.

6 Mount the work vertically in the vise and saw down to the shoulder lines as shown.

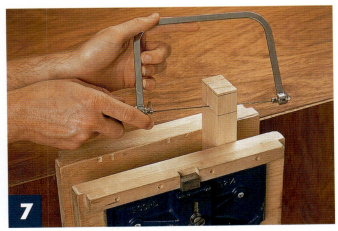

7 Remove the waste with a coping saw as shown, taking care not to go too close to the shoulder line. Whatever you leave will have to be removed with a chisel later. Check the back shoulder line repeatedly as you saw.

8 Use a sharp bevel-edge chisel to remove the remaining waste. Only chisel to just past the middle of the socket, then turn the work around and come in from the other side. Keep the tool level, and don't attempt to remove too much at one time. If you encounter any resistance, give a light tap with a mallet—don't use the palm of your hand!

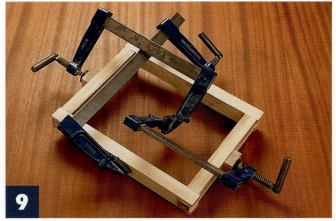

9

When all the joints have been cut, try a dry run. You may need to pare a small amount from the pins or the shoulders; if so, take the wood off with a chisel, a shaving at a time. When fitting the joints, do not force them in any way or you run the risk of splitting the sockets. When you have a perfect fit, lay the work on a flat surface and prepare to glue up. If your clamps are too short, use two in line. When dry, saw off the horns; take care not to mark the surface.

10

Scrape any glue residue from the inside the frame and lay it over the main block. Check for fit, then saw the waste from the block, using a jigsaw, hand saw, or circular saw. Adjust if necessary by planing the edge and the back face of the block, using a belt sander fitted with a flat sanding plate and finishing with a block plane. Glue the block inside the frame, using a liberal coating of glue. When dry, use a block plane on the end grain of the dovetails. Plane off a ¹⁄₁₆ in. (2 mm) arris from all sharp edges.

Knife Rack

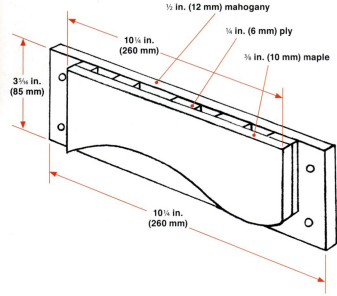

½ in. (12 mm) mahogany

¼ in. (6 mm) ply

10¼ in. (260 mm)

⅜ in. (10 mm) maple

3⁵⁄₁₆ in. (85 mm)

10¼ in. (260 mm)

Prepare the maple front and mahogany back as per the cutting list. Mark up by setting the bevel to 20 degrees and laying the stock across the end. Draw a curve freehand or by using a Flexicurve, shown here, or French curves, then cut with a jigsaw fitted with a fine blade. Use the maple as a template to copy the shape onto the plywood, and cut it out. The mahogany back needs a bevel at each end only.

Lay the plywood on the back and position all the knives that you intend to use in position. Use a sharp pencil to draw around them accurately, leaving a gap of approximately 1/64 in. (0.5 mm) from the blade. Make sure that you identify the waste wood by crosshatching to avoid confusion, and then cut the plywood into strips.

Lay the plywood over the back, spacing the knives as you go. Mark the outlines with a pencil. Using waterproof wood adhesive according to the manufacturer's instructions, glue up the workpiece as a sandwich. Clamp up using one centrally placed large G-clamp or two equally spaced smaller ones, checking continually that none of the plywood spacers has slipped.

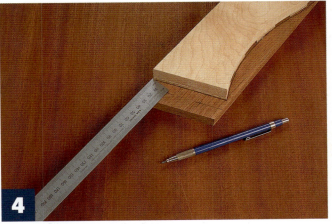

Let the assembly dry, preferably overnight. When it is completely dry, mark out four equally spaced 1/8 in. (3 mm) screw holes, using a ruler as a guide for spacing. Drill the holes using a countersink bit, and tidy the edges up if necessary. Finally, drill wall holes, insert wall plugs, and screw the rack to the wall at a 20-degree angle.

Traditional Cupboard

Making cabinets is easy with a router: fitting shelves, making paneled doors, and recessing of hinges are all easily accomplished. This small, wall-hung cabinet incorporates a traditional inset paneled door and an internal shelf.

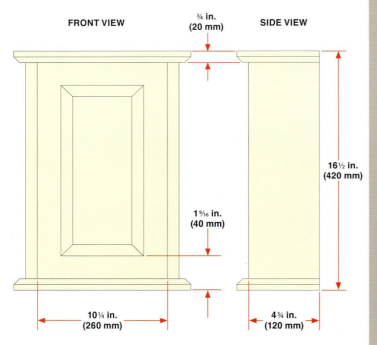

FRONT VIEW

SIDE VIEW

¾ in. (20 mm)

16½ in. (420 mm)

1 ⁹⁄₁₆ in. (40 mm)

10¼ in. (260 mm)

4¾ in. (120 mm)

Cut the top, base, and two sides to size. Mark the position of the sides on the top and base panels. They are set in ¾ in. (20 mm) from the end, and it is important to mark the position of the inside face. Transfer the markings across both panels.

Mark the center point of each of the sides on the outside face, using the combination square. Make sure that the mark is clear because this is what you will use to position the biscuit jointer. Place one of the sides on the base panel with the inside edge lined up with the marked line. Use the G-clamps to clamp it in position with the rear edges lined up.

The joint is cut with a biscuit jointer, using the base of the tool as the reference. Make sure that the depth is set for size 20 biscuits. Stand the jointer vertically and place it hard against the end of the clamped side board. Cut a slot. Leaving the boards clamped together, use the biscuit jointer horizontally, lined up on the same mark, and cut a slot in the end of the side. Repeat this process for all four corners.

The next job is to cut the rabbet to hold the back panel. This is simple to do on the sides. Fit the straight cutter in the router table and set the fence back so that the outside of the cutter is ¼ in. (6 mm) away. Set the height of the cutter to around ⅜ in. (10 mm). Mold the inside back edge of both sides.

Molding the top and base panels is trickier because the rabbets do not run for the full length. Mark the exact position of the ends of the rabbets by standing the sides in their correct positions on the end panels. Put biscuits in the joints to situate them accurately. Mark the end of the rabbet on the back of the base/top panel. Extend the line onto the underside/top of the panel.

Place the panel on the router table with the cutter set as before. You need to limit the travel of the board so that you do not make the rabbet too long. This is done by clamping stop blocks to the fence with the G-clamps. Set the panel on the table so that the front mark is just in front of the cutter. Clamp a block to the fence, hard up against the back of the board. Move the board forward and set it so that the rear mark is just behind the cutter. Now clamp another block to the fence, hard up against the front of the board.

To make the cut, start the router and hold the board at an angle against the rear stop block. Gently push it toward the cutter. As soon as it is flat against the fence, push it smoothly forward until it reaches the front stop block. Pull the rear of the board away from the cutter and turn off the router.

8 The completed rabbet. Square off the ends of the rabbet using a chisel.

9 Mold the inside faces of the top and base panels with the bearing-guided chamfer cutter. Set the fence in line with the cutter bearing and make a series of shallow passes, working around the board, starting on one end. Do not mold the back edge. After each pass, check the profile on the edge of the board. Keep raising the cutter for each pass until you are satisfied with the shape.

10 It is a good idea to roughly assemble the cabinet to make sure it looks good. Before assembling the cabinet permanently, rout out the recesses for the hinges. Set the hinges 1 9/16 in. (40 mm) in from the ends of the side panel. Mark their positions with a pencil. The hinge should be set into the board so that only half the knuckle protrudes.

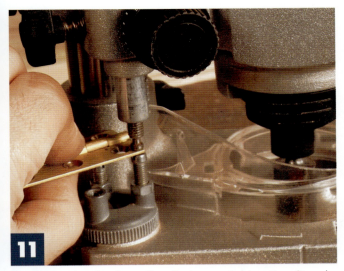

To set the depth of cut, first fit the straight cutter. Stand the router on a flat board and, with the motor off, plunge the cutter down so that it just touches the board. Now take an open hinge and place it on top of the depth-setting turret. Wind down the depth adjuster until it touches the top of the hinge. Lock the depth stop, and when you plunge the router, it will go to exactly the right depth.

Carefully rout out the waste, being careful not to go over the lines. It is actually easier to plunge the router and lock it down, then start the motor and feed the cutter into the lumber and move it along the edge between the marked lines. The side fence should be set to the width of the hinge leaf. Square off the ends of the completed recess with a chisel.

Next cut the housing for the internal shelf. This is a "stopped" housing that does not run the full width of the board. Mark out the position of the housing with a line across the center of both side boards. Mark a point 1 in. (25 mm) back from the front edge of each board. This is the place where the housing will end. Lay the two boards back to back on a workbench, and clamp a pair of battens across both boards in order to guide the router along the marked line. Make sure that the battens are parallel to each other and the marked line.

The router will sandwich itself neatly between the battens. The housing depth should be about ¼ in. (6 mm). Be careful not to run over the end lines.

15

After routing the housings, square off the ends with a chisel. The cabinet frame is now ready to assemble. Do not try to fit the shelf now, but wait until the frame is complete. Apply glue to the biscuit joints and the board ends, and clamp up the assembly tightly with the bar clamps. Make sure that the cabinet is square and leave to dry.

16

Measure into the housings and cut the shelf to length. Plane it to the correct thickness so that it slides into the frame. Apply a little glue to fix it in position. Cut the back panel to size and fit it into the rabbet. Do not fix in place yet because you may want to remove it later to make it easier to fit the door catch.

17

To make the paneled door, you will need a dedicated profile/scriber cutter set. These cutters will mold the doorframe, cut the joints, and also mold the edge of the central panel.

Before routing, the components must be cut to size. Measure the opening on the front of the cabinet and cut the two stiles (the uprights), so that they fit exactly. Place them in position and measure the space between them. The length of the rails (crosspieces) should be this measurement plus an allowance for the length of the joints on their ends. First, cut the tenons on the end of the rails. Set the cutter to the correct height so that the tenon will be in the right position.

Set the fence exactly in line with the guide bearing on the cutter. Use a metal ruler to ensure it is correct.

Molding end grain must be done with care, and because the rails on this door are particularly short, added precautions are necessary. To hold the rail at right angles to the cutter, use a wide board behind it. Press the ends of both boards up against the fence and clamp them together as shown in the picture. The rails are routed face up on the table. Repeat the process on both ends of each rail.

The cutter must now be reset to cut the profile and the groove on the inside edge of the doorframe. On this cutter set, this is done simply by raising the cutter in the table. Place the rail face down on the table next to the cutter. Raise the cutter until the edge of the slotting cutter is exactly level with the tenon. This setting is critical to achieving a good joint.

The stiles and rails are molded on their inside edges and are placed face down on the table. Again, the shortness of the rails makes it difficult to mold them safely by hand, so take a piece of plywood or MDF and cut out a section to hold the rail. Use this to run the rail safely past the cutter. The doorframe should fit neatly together once all the routing has been done.

Now the panel must be machined to fit the frame. Assemble the frame and measure the size into the grooves. Subtract ³⁄₁₆ in. (4 mm) from the width and ¹⁄₁₆ in. (2 mm) from the height and cut the panel to this size. A panel-raising cutter is used to cut the profile around the panel. This is a large-diameter cutter, which must be run at a slow speed—generally around 12,000 rpm.

Work around the panel, starting on the end grain, and make shallow passes. Take your time on this because it is important to produce a good finish. Raise the cutter a little after each pass. This obviously makes the edge thinner. Carry on until the panel is thin enough to slip into the groove in the doorframe. It should be tight enough not to rattle, but not so tight that it jams.

25

Assemble the door dry (without glue) to test it, using bar clamps and making sure that all the joints fit snugly and the panel is secure. Dismantle, apply glue to the joints, and reassemble. Be careful not to get any glue in the panel grooves—the panel must be free to move, otherwise it may split. Clamp up tightly and leave to dry.

26

The door will need a little adjustment before it fits the cabinet properly. Plane the sides evenly until it will fit the cabinet with a gap of approximately 1/32 in. (1 mm) on all sides.

27

Fit the hinges in the cabinet and attach with one screw each. Open the hinges and stand the door in position in the cabinet. Fold a piece of sandpaper and place it under the corner of the door to lift it off the base panel. Fold the hinges over the front of the door and mark their position with a pencil.

28

Fit the door into the bench vise and transfer the pencil marks onto the back edge. Rout out the hinge recesses using exactly the same settings used on the cabinet side. Be very careful to hold the router level on the door edge, because there is not a great deal of support and it is easy to let it tip. Square off the ends of the recesses after routing. Temporarily fit the door with one screw per hinge and check the fit. Remove and make any necessary adjustments. When you are happy with the fit and the door shows an even gap on all sides, carefully fit all the screws and tighten. Fit a knob and a catch to hold the door shut. Finally, fix the back in place with hammer and panel pins.

Modernist Cupboard

This project is essentially a variation on a theme. The lumber used for the doors, which are hung on an existing cupboard unit, is the highly fashionable maple, which is straight-grained and satisfying to work. Low-voltage lights are mounted inside the cupboards; if you wish to do this you will need to bring an electric feed up to the top of the cupboard. The transformer can be left just sitting above the cupboard, with the fittings mounted in the top.

You can use glass doors fitted at low level for floor units, although I wouldn't recommend them if you have young children. Frosted glass blurs the cupboard's contents and is a compromise between to display or to conceal. If the contents are very much display items, use clear glass or, for a truly modernist look, Georgian wired safety glass.

In this project, it is assumed that you have mastered the skills required to true up your lumber and that you are reasonably competent at making a mortise and tenon joint. The joint used in this door is a haunched mortise and tenon with ½ in. (12 mm) cut away, so that the rabbet for the glass does not expose the tenon.

Essential Tools & Materials

Tools

- pencil
- straightedge
- measuring tape
- square
- marking gauge
- mortise gauge
- marking knife
- screwdriver
- jack plane
- block plane
- ¼ in., ½ in., and 1 in. (6 mm, 12 mm, and 25 mm) bevel-edge chisels
- mallet
- backsaw (tenon saw)
- drill, drill stand
- router, 1⅜ in. (35 mm) recessed hinge cutter, router, ¼ in. (6 mm) straight cutter, ⅜ in. (10 mm) rabbet cutter with guide wheel
- workbench
- sash clamps
- table-mounted circular saw (optional)

Hardware etc.

- 23 15/16 x 15 in. (608 x 382 mm) etched or sandblasted 3/16 in. (4 mm) glass
- molding pins
- PVA wood glue
- sandpaper in grits 100 to 300

Wood

- (These quantities are for one door with a finished size of 28⅜ x 19 11/16 in. (720 x 500 mm); multiply these amounts or alter the lengths as necessary)
- 2 pieces 29⅛ x 2½ x 11/16 in. (740 x 65 x 18 mm) maple
- 2 pieces 20½ x 2½ x 11/16 in. (520 x 65 x 18 mm) maple
- 78¾ x ¼ x ¼ in. (2000 mm x 6 mm x 6 mm) hardwood fillet

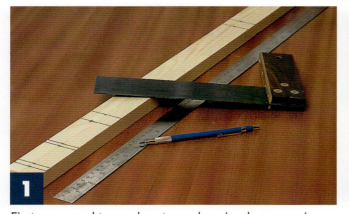

1

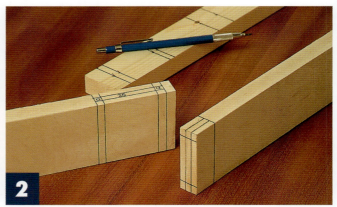

2

First, you need to mark out a rod, a simple measuring stick with all the dimensions to be transferred to each piece of lumber. Starting at one end of the rod, mark an end point. Measure from this the height of your doors and mark them for the upright pieces, called stiles. In this photo, the line in the foreground on the rod is the end point; next, ½ in. (12 mm) along, is the line marking the haunch of the tenon, then the line of the cut back for the glass rabbet, and then the line for the full width of the rail that will meet up to the stile. The horizontal boards of a door are called rails and, because they are so much shorter, you can mark them between the stile marks. Normally all marks would start from the same end point, but to avoid visual confusion, they are placed in the middle. The final line in the foreground, just in front of the square, is the length of the tenon.

Line up all your stiles, cut them about 1 ³⁄₁₆ in. (30 mm) longer than the finished length and transfer the marks from the rod. Repeat this for the rails, but note that these will need to be cut exactly to length. Mark the mortises and tenons with a mortise gauge; when fully marked out at both ends, they should look as shown here. The tenon marking is to the foreground, with the mortise marking out behind it. The rod is shown to the rear.

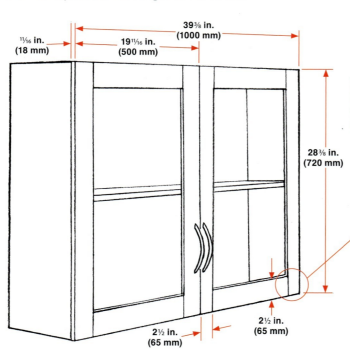

The diagram above gives the correct measurements for the haunched mortise and tenon joint.

If you have good control of a caulking gun, it is possible to fix the glass in the cupboard doors by running a small bead of clear caulk around the inside of the glass.

Use a router with a ¼ in. (6 mm) bit to chop the mortises, remembering that the haunches are only cut to ½ in. (12 mm) deep. Clean up the rounded ends of the mortise with a ¼ in. (6 mm) chisel. If you have two fences for your router, one fixed to each side of the workpiece is a great help. Because the mortise in this project are cut with a router and the greatest safe depth of cut—1 ³/₁₆ in. (30 mm)—is shorter than normal, the tenons will also need to be cut to this shorter length. It is, however, perfectly adequate for this size door.

4 Cut the cheeks and haunches with a tenon saw or a router; if you use the latter, use a guide and a block the same thickness as the workpiece to give additional support.

Dry-assemble, making sure that the frame is lying flat on the clamps, and check the frame for square— each measurement from corner to corner should be exactly the same. If not, adjust by moving one of the sash clamps slightly out of parallel, and retighten it.

When dry, remove the frame from the clamps and lay it on the workbench. Secure and rout out the glazing rabbet to a depth of ½ in. (12 mm), using a rabbet cutter with a guide wheel that will remove a ⅜ in. (10 mm) rabbet. If you are experienced at marking out, you may wish to do this step prior to following step 5. If not, doing it at this stage makes it much easier to work out what is happening. The cutter will leave radiused corners, which must be cut square with a chisel before you fit the glass.

The quickest method to mark the hinge positions is to use the old door you have already removed. Lay the doors edge to edge and transfer the marks, ensuring that the center is the same distance from the edge as in the old door.

Mount your drill in a drill stand and cut the holes for the hinges to the correct depth using a recessed hinge cutter; in this case, the depth was ½ in. (12 mm). You can use a router fitted with a 1 ⅜ in. (35 mm) cutter to cut the hinge holes, but it is worth balancing up the cost of buying an expensive router cutter against that of a far cheaper drill cutter. Fit the glass using small maple fillets fixed in place with molding pins. Hang the doors and adjust them by careful setting of the hinge adjusting screws.

Picture Rail Shelf

This simple shelving system can be attached to the walls of a room by wall plugs and screws, giving you a fashionable display and storage space that is quick and easy to construct. The height will vary according to the ceiling height of your room, but about 11 13/16 in. (300 mm) above head height would be normal. It may also be fixed at dado rail height, about 31 7/16 in. (800 mm) from the floor.

Normally, the shelf would be fixed around all the walls, with breaks for any windows or doors. When measuring the length you'll need to take into account any external miters that need to be cut; in a modern house the rooms are usually rectangular, with no external miters required, but in older houses you may have a chimney breast protruding into the room, which will require a miter on either side. All the internal angles are simple butt joints. The pegs are fixed at 11 13/16 in. (300 mm) centers here, but they can be at any regular spacing. Note that the pegs are slightly angled upward, at 80 degrees to the face of the support, to stop things falling off them.

The lumber is softwood that is then primed and undercoated prior to fixing, and is finished with eggshell paint when in place.

Essential Tools & Materials

Tools
- pencil
- measuring tape
- combination square
- sliding bevel
- screwdriver
- miter saw
- drill, 1 in. (25 mm) hole saw or flat bit, 3/16 in. (4 mm) wood bit, countersink bit
- 1 in. (25 mm) bevel-edge chisel
- mallet
- block plane
- workbench
- level

Hardware etc.
- 2 in. (50 mm) x No. 8 countersink screws
- PVA wood glue
- sandpaper in grits 80 and 150

Wood
- 2 pieces 4 x 1 in. (100 x 25 mm) x the circumference of your room plus 10 percent straight-grained pine or similar (S4S)
- 1 in. (25 mm) diameter broomstick or hardwood dowel
- small scrap pieces of hardwood for wedges

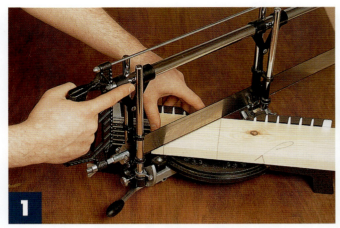

2 Transfer the measurement, allowing for the different reduction, to the matching support part and cut as demonstrated before.

1 Cut the 4 x 1 in. (100 x 25 mm) lumber into two lengths, one for the shelf and one for the support. When calculating the lengths, start in one corner of the room and work your way around. The first support will be the full extent of the wall, but subsequent ones will be shorter by the thickness of the proceeding one; the shelf measurement will also reduce by the width of the preceding one. The easiest method of cutting a miter is to mark the actual length of the wall on the shelf, taking into account any reduction, then square across the lumber and mark the miter along the face using a combination square. Cut using a miter saw or a miter block and backsaw (tenon saw).

3 Calculate the number of pegs and cut one to length. Measure this one, mark it for use as your pattern, and then use the pattern as a template. You could cut the pegs to 5 15/16 in. (150 mm), which projects past the front of the shelf, or shorter, giving you more pegs per length of dowel. It is probably inadvisable to make the pegs any shorter than 3 1/8 in. (80 mm).

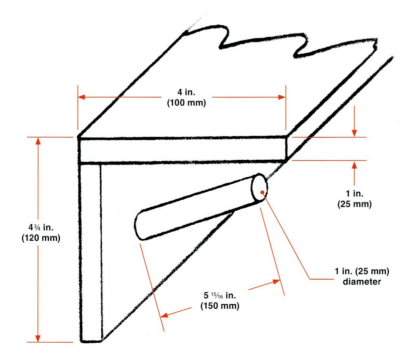

4 in.
(100 mm)

1 in.
(25 mm)

4¾ in.
(120 mm)

5 15/16 in.
(150 mm)

1 in. (25 mm)
diameter

Inspired by the simple, elegant designs of Shaker craftsmen, this rail can be used anywhere.

4

Mark out the position of the pegs at your chosen centers, with the hole centers a little below the centerline of the face side. Hold a peg in place and visually adjust the angle that you want the peg to incline. Check that you will have enough space to clear the underside of the shelf; 1 ⅜ in. (35 mm) is an average. Secure the workpiece, use a sliding bevel set to the angle of incline of the pegs as a guide, and then drill the peg holes using a hole cutter or a flat bit drill. As you drill, be careful of any splitting out at the back.

5

Smear each peg with a little glue and insert it into the hole. Let the peg pass through the back of the support until the lower edge just meets the rear face. Ensure that the peg is supported underneath and sharply tap the end grain with a chisel. This will split the peg, allowing you to knock in a small, shallow hardwood wedge, as shown.

6

Be careful that you do not tap the wedges too hard, otherwise you may split the end grain of the peg further than the face of the support. Let the glue dry, preferably overnight, then use a saw to cut the peg and wedges almost flush with the rear face. Finish by planing the peg and wedges flush to the back of the support with a block plane. As always when planing end grain, apply pressure to the toe of the block plane and make sure that the blade is very sharp before you start.

7

Drill and countersink the shelf components through the back edge at a regular center of about 15 ¾ in. (400 mm). Match each shelf to its support, glue along the edge of the support, and fasten with 2 in. (50 mm) screws. Keep the two parts together at 90 degrees, and be careful that the screws do not come through the face or the back of the support. Sand lightly, then prime.

Kitchen Sink Makeover

You can transform most kitchens with a little time, money, and ingenuity. This "makeover" retains the basic kitchen unit carcass, and replaces the doors, drawer fronts, and countertop with your own custom-made versions. Most fitted kitchens are made from coated particleboard, which chips easily and becomes swollen and bloated when subject to moisture. Pay special attention to the sink cupboard: you may need to replace the whole thing, in which case buy from a cheaper range and discard the doors and false drawer fronts. If any part is swollen or the coating is damaged, replace it.

All doors and drawer fronts should be replaced with painted MDF or solid lumber, and the work surfaces replaced with plywood covered in a waterproof material: tiles, slate, resin, or even real wood. This project uses 11 13/16 in. (300 mm) square ceramic floor tiles, cemented to low-grade construction plywood using flexible tile cement.

The sinks are stainless steel inset bowls with a monoblock mixer faucet serving both. If you need to move the sink, you will have to sort out the new feed for the faucets and a drain pipe. Plan and complete any electrical work first. If you need additional sockets and have any doubt whatsoever about your competence, hire a qualified electrician.

To finish, use eggshell paint after priming and undercoating the MDF. It's easiest to remove the doors for painting.

Essential Tools & Materials

Tools
- pencil
- straightedge
- measuring tape
- square
- screwdriver
- caulking gun
- panel saw
- jigsaw
- electric drill, 3/16 in. (4 mm) twist bit, 1 3/8 in. (35 mm) recessed hinge cutter, drill stand
- jack plane
- block plane
- workbench with vise
- For cutting ceramic tiles: tile cutter, angle grinder with stone-cutting disc, hacksaw frame with ceramic cutting file fitted
- table-mounted or handheld circular saw (optional)

Hardware etc.
- ceramic tiles and flexible tile cement
- inset sink(s) and taps
- drawer and door handles
- silicone caulk
- plastic corner blocks
- 30 11/16 in. (18 mm) x No. 6 brass countersink screws
- sandpaper in grits 80 and 100

Wood
- 21 13/16 x 19 11/16 x 9/16 in. (554 x 500 x 15 mm) MDF per door
- 8 13/16 x 19 11/16 x 9/16 in. (224 x 500 x 15 mm) MDF per drawer
- 88 3/16 x 48 x 11/16 in. (2440 x 1220 x 18 mm) shuttering plywood
- 78 3/4 x 3/4 x 1 in. (2000 x 20 x 25 mm) hardwood lipping

Countertops

Remove the existing countertop and sink, which will be attached with angle brackets underneath. If you have pipes running through the countertop, these will have to be cut free. Repeat the shape of the old countertop in the shuttering plywood and fit in place, using new brackets if necessary. If you need to join the plywood, make the join meet over the place where two adjacent cupboards abut. Most manufacturers provide a paper template to cut the hole(s) for a new sink; drill a small hole to start the cut and then follow the line with a jigsaw.

Loosely lay out the tiles on the countertop, allowing a ³⁄₁₆ in. (4 mm) grout line between all joins; find a visual balance that keeps cutting to a minimum. Where possible, any cuts should be placed to the back or the sides of the countertop. It's a good idea to have a join running through where the faucet hole will be. This will also give a neat line through the middle of the two sinks. Mark the tiles with a felt pen and cut them as shown. To cut curved tiles, transfer the sink cutout to the tile and then clamp the tile securely. Tape over the good part of the tile with masking tape to protect it should you slip, and run around the curved line with an angle grinder. If you haven't done this before, take it slowly. When you have ground down about halfway, the waste will break off and you will be left with a very sharp jagged edge. Use the grinder to smooth this off. When the tiles are cut, loose-lay them in position, check that the sink will fit, and adjust if needed.

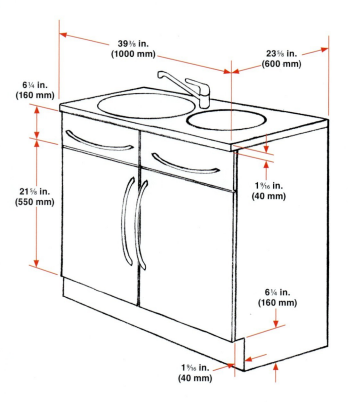

39 ³⁄₈ in.
(1000 mm)

23 ⁵⁄₈ in.
(600 mm)

6 ¼ in.
(160 mm)

21 ⁵⁄₈ in.
(550 mm)

1 ⁹⁄₁₆ in.
(40 mm)

6 ¼ in.
(160 mm)

1 ⁹⁄₁₆ in.
(40 mm)

TIP

Wear gardening gloves while handling the sharp edges of tiles; this will minimize the risk of accidents.

The dimensions shown in this diagram are compatible with most self-assembly sink units available at DIY shops. You can adapt the measurements to fit existing or one-off units, but make sure that you keep everything in proportion.

Spread the cement evenly on the back of each tile and twist into place. Some cement manufacturers recommend trowelling the surface to be attached to; when dealing with large tiles it is cleaner, if a little slower, to trowel onto the back of the tile. Use the cement applicator to ensure an even coating. Use tile spacers or matchsticks to keep an even grout line, and continually check the surface height, tapping down or adding cement as necessary.

When the tile cement is dry, usually the following day, cut and fit the edge beading. This should be the width of the tiles plus the plywood and about $5/16$–$1/2$ in. (8–12 mm) thick. Miter all the corners and screw in place. If you wish, you can counterbore and plug the screw holes. Grout the work surface and allow it to dry.

Place the sinks into the holes, seal with silicone caulk, and tighten the sink clamps from underneath the countertop, according to the manufacturer's instructions. As you tighten the screws, the caulk will be expelled from under the sink rim; wipe away any excess with a wet finger, using clean water from a bowl, not your saliva. Fit and connect the faucets, using flexible hose connectors if you're a weekend plumber. The sink waste will need to be adapted if you are changing from one sink to a two-bowl system. A simple dimensioned sketch will be enough to solve your problem if you take it to a good plumbing supply store. Buy the push-fit waste system, not the glued type.

Drawer Fronts and Doors

1 Remove each door and drawer from the existing units and lay it over a sheet of ⁹⁄₁₆ in. (15 mm) MDF. Mark around each component, using the board to the most economical advantage. Remember to allow for the thickness of your saw cut (the kerf) when marking. If any of your existing doors are damaged in any way, do not use them as a template, but substitute another of the same size.

2 Ensure that the board is firmly supported and fix a batten as a guide, then saw the components off—using a circular saw makes the job easy. Stack them in groups of the same size, clamp in a vise, and plane the edges smooth and square. You may wish to put a slight bevel on the face edges at this stage, using a block plane: about ³⁄₁₆ in. (4 mm) all around looks attractive.

3 Attach a corner block at each end of the false drawer fronts and place in position on the cupboard. Inset the blocks by the thickness of the uprights, half the thickness in the center of a double unit. Make sure that the drawer front is square and level, then screw it in place. (Use a awl to start the screws off.) If replacing any practical (functional) drawers, simply unscrew the old front from inside the drawer and replace with your new version. With regard to fitting the doors, refer to step 10.

4 The handles come with an attaching template, and the only thing to be done is to choose their placing. Center the drawer handles on the width of the drawer; a low placing looks better for the drawer handles. The door handles are placed 2 in. (50 mm) in from the edge and lifted toward the top, partly for ergonomic reasons and partly for a visual balance. Play around with the placing until you feel satisfied that the handles are in the best position in relation to each other. When you have decided, attach all handles in exactly the same position, ensuring that they are exactly square. To cut the holes for the door hinges, see page 175, steps 7 and 8.

5 You will have to spend some time adjusting the fit of the doors; it is tedious but straightforward. There are usually two adjusting screws on each hinge: the larger allows you to move the hinge forward on the hinge backplate. By adjusting each of the pair of hinges using these screws, as shown, you can get the hinge edge of the door square to the edge of the cupboard. The smaller screw, often hidden inside the plastic casing, allows you to "throw the door forward," adjusting the other edge. This is important if you have a pair of doors meeting, because the gap between them must be parallel and the tops at the same height.

Projects for Storage

186 Shelf Unit

192 "Waney" Shelves

196 Stackable Storage Units

200 Corner Cupboard

Shelf Unit

A fundamental rule of good design is the rule of conceal and display: conceal the unattractive, and display—with verve—the attractive!

This shape works best when hung between two ordinary wall units. It breaks up the rigid lines of most fitted kitchens, for example, and allows the eye to be caught by the display. Use ½ in. (12 mm) board for the shelf dividers, because the difference in the thickness between the dividers and the ⁹⁄₁₆ in. (15 mm) shelves provides a balance that works well visually. Note also that the end of the front curve passes in front of the sides; this requires some tinkering to mark out, but it will give your shelves a far slicker look.

As always, wear a dust mask when working with MDF, especially when working with power tools. The finish used here is eggshell paint but you could use emulsion, maybe picking out the leading edge of the shelves in a complementary tone, finishing with matte varnish.

Essential Tools & Materials

Tools
- pencil
- steel ruler or measuring tape
- square
- string
- panel saw
- router, ½ in. (12 mm) and ⁹⁄₁₆ in. (15 mm) straight cutters
- jigsaw
- face mask
- drill, ⅛ in. (3 mm) twist bit
- screwdrivers
- ½ in. (12 mm) bevel-edge chisel
- mallet
- jack plane
- 2 sash clamps or clamp heads
- two 11 ¹³⁄₁₆ in. (300 mm) G-clamps
- workbench with vise
- beam compass (optional)
- circular saw (optional)
- cordless screwdriver (optional)
- belt sander (optional)

Hardware etc.
- 16 zinc-plated countersink screws 2 in. (50 mm) x No. 6
- PVA wood glue
- sandpaper in grits 80 to 240
- woodfiller
- 4 large mirror plates with attaching screws

Wood
- 48 x 48 x ⁹⁄₁₆ in. (1220 x 1220 x 15 mm) MDF
- 48 x 9¹⁄₁₆ x ½ in. (1220 x 230 x 12 mm) MDF

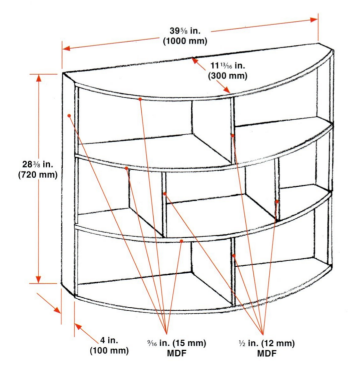

The dimensions in this diagram are as for a standard double wall unit of 39⅝ x 28⅜ in. (1000 x 720 mm), but you can alter the height as required. Other standard heights are 23⅝ x 21⅝ in. (600 and 550 mm).

1

Measure 39⅝ in. (1000 mm) from the best MDF edge along two sides of the board. Join the marks, find the center, mark the top and bottom, and draw another line parallel to the first. Draw a line 11 ¹³⁄₁₆ in. (300 mm) from the front of the board at 90 degrees to the other two lines. This line should stop at the 39⅝ in. (1000 mm) line drawn first. Use a beam compass or string and pencil to scribe a 28⅜ in. (720 mm) radius arc; the distance from the outer edge of the arc to the back of the shelf should be 4 in. (100 mm). Cut, leaving the line on the larger piece, then true up with your plane.

2

Use a jigsaw to cut away the waste from the front of your shelf, making sure that the work is well supported and that there is no likelihood of your cutting into the workbench. Use a handsaw or a circular saw to cut the back of this first shelf, and plane or sand the edges as true as you can. This shelf will now be your pattern for the other three and should be marked up accordingly in the steps below.

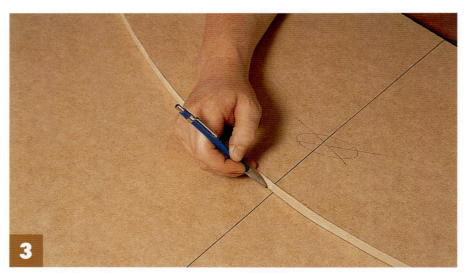

3

Lay the shelf back on the board, ensuring that the centerline is in line with the centerline drawn on the board at both the front and back. The ends should be also in the correct place. Carefully draw around your pattern shelf. Repeat steps 2 and 3 for the remaining shelves.

4

Place all four shelves together in your vise, ensuring that the centerline that you drew in step 1 is showing on the front and back of the two outside shelves. Clamp the ends in such a way that you do not interrupt the passage of your plane, and then plane the back edges flat, as shown.

5

You will now need to mark the housings for the uprights. You need three lines: first, the centerline already visible. Transfer this across the backs of all four shelves. Next, measure out from the centerline 9⅞ in. (250 mm) to both the left and right. Draw a line across the backs, squaring the line down the faces of the two outer shelves. Finally, measure ¼ in. (6 mm) on either side of all three lines. Square these marks across the backs and down the front of the outer shelves.

6

◄ Keeping the clamps in place, release the shelves from the vise and turn them around with the curved front edges uppermost. Finish these edges with a belt sander or a sharp plane, working from each end toward the middle. As you work, check the front edges for square, correcting as necessary. Release the shelves from the vise and clamps. Mark each shelf to identify it: "top," "upper middle," "lower middle," and "bottom." The top shelf has one centrally placed housing on the underside; mark it accordingly. The upper middle shelf has one housing on the top in the center but two offset on its underside; use one of the shelves that were on the outside when they were in the vise, as they will already have the two outer housings marked on it. Finally set your marking gauge to ¾ in. (20 mm) and run it across the front end of each housing. The housings are "stopped housings," so you will not see them from the front when the unit is assembled.

7

8

Set up your router to cut a ½ in. (12 mm) housing to a depth of ³⁄₁₆ in. (10 mm), and use a fence clamped to the shelf. Make sure that the clamp is firmly attached and will not move, then run the router along the fence until you reach the mark made by the marking gauge in step 6. Repeat for each housing on all the shelves.

Now cut the ends of your shelves to allow the front edge to pass over the front edge of the sides. For the middle two shelves the process is to mark a line ⁹⁄₁₆ in. (15 mm) in from each end, square from the back of the shelves, then a second line square from the point where the arc meets the end. Remove this 4 x ⁹⁄₁₆ in. (100 x 15 mm) portion with a hand- or jigsaw. Repeat the marking-out on the underside of the top shelf and on the top of the bottom shelf. Remove these two portions with the router to a depth of ³⁄₁₆ in. (10 mm), using a ⁹⁄₁₆ in. (15 mm) cutter and a fence set up as before; stop when you reach the line from the end of the arc.

9

Clean up the stopped ends with a sharp chisel. Retrieve the scrap piece from step 1, then mark it twice to 4 x 27 ¹⁵⁄₁₆ in. (100 x 710 mm) for the sides. Cut the scrap piece and run a plane over the saw cuts to tidy them up. Next take the ½ in. (12 mm) MDF and cut the uprights: two at 11 ¹³⁄₁₆ x 9 ¹⁄₁₆ in. (300 x 230 mm) and two at 10¼ x 9⅛ in. (260 x 230 mm). Mark and cut the waste for the stopped housings as shown, to ³⁄₁₆ in. (10 mm) deep and ¾ in. (20 mm) long on the top and bottom of each upright. (The 9¹⁄₁₆ in. [230 mm] is the height.)

TIPS

To ensure that you have measured the correct distance from the edge of your router baseplate to the fence, do a test cut on a piece of waste before starting to cut in earnest. To check the alignment, run the router over the cut with the cutter lowered and the motor switched off.

10 Clear your workbench and lay the shelves out in order on their back edges. One by one, place the uprights in place, the deeper uprights in the center of the top and bottom shelves, and the shallow ones offset between the two middle shelves. Place the side panels in place and get the whole assembly approximately square. Fix a batten down to the bench to hold the bottom shelf in place, fix another batten about 1 3/16 in. (30 mm) away from and parallel to the top shelf, then push a set of folding wedges in place. Repeat for the sides. Place your clamps and folding wedges in position with scrap wood as protection, and use them to pull everything into square. If the backs of the shelves are not sitting tight up against the uprights, use a scrap piece to force them together. When everything fits and is square, mark the centers of the shelf ends where they meet the sides.

11 Dismantle the assembly, square down from the marks on the side panels, and drill two 1/8 in. (3 mm) holes in each line. Apply PVA glue to all joints, including the shelf ends, and reassemble. Replace the clamps, wedges, and scrap pieces, recheck for square both internally and externally, and drive the 2 in. (50 mm) screws into the holes drilled in the side panels.

12 Wipe away excess glue with a damp rag, leave overnight to dry, and then release the wedges and clamps. If any screws are not driven below the surface, withdraw them, countersink the holes, and drive them in again. Fill over the screw heads with filler, then plane the front of the uprights to suit the arc of the shelves, planing toward the center. Finally, sand the edges and the filler over the screws, and paint as required. Use two mirror plates on each of the top and bottom shelves to attach the unit to the wall.

"Waney" Shelves

"Waney" or "waney edge" means lumber with the bark attached to one or more faces. Walnut is used here, but long, straight planks with a waney surface on the front edge work, too.

Cutting and finishing the shelves is not difficult; the cunning part is the hidden wall mounting. Use ⅜ in. (10 mm) diameter stainless steel rods inserted in the back edge, and then car body filler to go into both the shelf and the wall. If fitting into a corner, a nylon connecting block can be recessed into the edge to provide additional support. This method is fairly straightforward if you are attaching to a brick or stone wall, but if you live in a timber-framed house or you want to hang these shelves from a stud partition wall, a different approach must be taken.

Remove the plaster or dry wall lining from the attaching areas, from the other side of the wall. Drill through the exposed timber uprights with a ⅜ in. (10 mm) drill, insert ⅜ in. (10 mm) threaded rods, fix the rods into the shelf with body filler, and when dry, tighten up the nuts from the other side and cut the rods flush to the nut's surface. Plaster over the holes and make good.

Essential Tools & Materials

Tools
- pencil
- straightedge
- measuring tape
- square
- level
- half-round file
- electric drill, ⅜ in. (10 mm) wood bit, ⅜ in. (9 mm) masonry bit
- jigsaw
- jack plane
- block plane
- cabinet scraper
- workbench
- router with straight cutter (if fitting connecting block side support)

Hardware etc.
- ⅜ in. (10 mm) diameter stainless steel rod, about 7⅞ in. (125 mm) for every fixing point
- Two-part "elastic" car body filler
- Sandpaper in grits 60 to 240

Wood
- Hardwood with an interesting grain and at least one waney edge. It will need to be purchased with a specific site in mind, and this will determine the length and width, but the finished thickness should be about 1 to 1⅜ in. (25 to 35 mm)

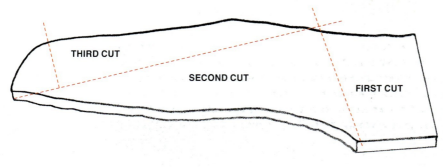

THIRD CUT SECOND CUT FIRST CUT

Check the angle at which your walls meet first—they may not be at right angles.

"Waney" Shelves

1 Select the board, assess the most advantageous shape to cut, and mark it out carefully. This triangular piece had a waney edge on both edges, with a sawn edge to the right-hand side. Cut across the grain at the wider end. If the shelves are to be part of a set when attached, consider the overall shape, the direction and coloring, of the grain and, most importantly, the curves and edge bevels.

2 Slice off the bulk of the bark with a chisel, and use a belt sander with a coarse belt to rapidly remove all the remaining fibrous matter, or phloem. You can use the nose of the tool to follow the undulations of the lumber. Plane the straight edges and the two faces and finish them with a cabinet scraper as normal.

3 Drill ⅜ in. (10 mm) diameter holes along the back edge of each shelf—around 11 ¹³/₁₆–15 ¾ in. (300–400 mm) between each center should be sufficient. The rods need to go into the shelf at least 4 in. (100 mm) deep. Use a square to assist you in keeping your drill perpendicular, and if your shelf is tapered, be careful to avoid breakout on the front edge where the shelf narrows.

4 Scribe the shelves to get an exact fit up to the wall. This is particularly important if you decide to use a support method as outlined on page 192. The greater the area of contact with the wall, the better your attaching will be. Use a level when marking the wall, and then use this line to scribe to. At the same time, mark another line on the wall for the underside of the shelf.

5

6

Each steel rod should be ⅜ in. (10 mm) shorter than the hole drilled into the back edge of your shelves, plus a minimum of 4 in. (100 mm) into the wall. The deeper you can go into the wall, the better, because the shelf will be stronger. Attach your drill to a bench vise, insert the rods, and use a file as shown to round off each end slightly. Also cut a "key" along the length of each rod. This will assist the filler in bonding with the stainless steel.

If you are hanging the shelves in an alcove or a corner, a way to achieve even greater hidden support is to rout out a channel in the side edge of each shelf. This should be of sufficient width and depth to receive half a nylon connector block. Start the channel about 3⅛ in. (80 mm) from the back of the shelf, and stop it just short of the front.

7 Insert the rods into the back edge and carefully mark the wall between the upper and lower lines. Drill out the wall using an undersized bit, in this case ⅜ in. (9 mm) for a brick wall; concrete or stone will require a full-sized ⅜ in. (10 mm) bit.

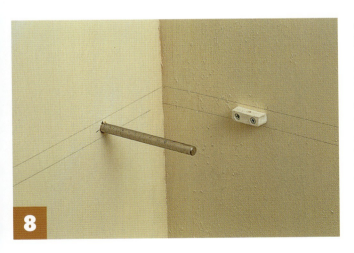

8

◄ Mark for the connector block, if used. It needs to be sited the length of the protruding rods, plus ⅜ in. (10 mm) forward from the back wall. The rods can then be inserted into the wall, and when the shelf is pushed back into place, the nylon block will slide along its channel until the shelf is fully in place. Hammer home the rods. Coat the wall, the protruding rods, and the back edge and holes of the shelf with filler and push the shelf home. Do a dry run, and only apply the filler when you are sure everything fits. Clean off any excess filler with a sharp knife before it has set fully.

TIP

To ensure that the shelves will fit when cut, make a small cardboard model at 1:10 or 1:12 scale beforehand.

Stackable Storage Units

A simple method of securely jointing the thin boards used in this project is to use finger joints. These are castellations running along the end of one board, with a similar set cut into the adjacent board. For the better equipped workshop, especially if you see yourself wanting to make any quantity of lightweight plywood furniture or storage boxes, it's a good idea to invest in a template cutter; this project uses a finger joint template. With a template such as this, it is possible to cut two boards of up to 11 $^{13}/_{16}$ in. (300 mm) wide at once, ranged side by side; however, for the sake of clarity here it is shown being used just on one side. When you have mastered this simple jointing technique the possibilities are endless, enabling you to make a wide range of modern furniture simply, quickly, and maybe profitably!

The internal dimensions will be governed by what you intend to store: the antiqued baskets shown here can be obtained in a wide range of sizes. But a further consideration could well be the dimensions of your stereo or video, etc. Just draw out the external dimensions of the items, add $^3/_{16}$ in. (10 mm) on each side, top and bottom, and twice the thickness of the plywood to obtain the outside dimensions of the unit.

Essential Tools & Materials

Tools
- pencil
- steel ruler or measuring tape
- square
- marking knife
- circular saw
- router, $^5/_{16}$ in. and $^3/_8$ in. (8 mm and 9.5 mm) straight cutters, dovetail cutting jig with finger-jointing plate to suit your router
- $^1/_4$ in. (6 mm) and $^3/_8$ in. (9 mm) bevel-edge chisels
- jack plane
- block plane
- sash clamps
- workbench

Hardware etc.
- PVA wood glue
- $^3/_4$ in. (20 mm) molding pins
- sandpaper grades 100 and 150

Wood
- 88$^3/_{16}$ x 48 x $^3/_8$ in. (2440 x 1220 x 9.5 mm) birch-faced plywood (boxes)
- 48 x 31$^7/_{16}$ x $^1/_4$ in. (1220 x 800 x 6 mm) MDF or plywood (backs)

Cutting list per unit
- 2 pieces 31$^7/_{16}$ x 9$^7/_{16}$ x $^3/_8$ in. (800 x 240 x 9.5 mm) (top and base)
- 2 pieces 15$^3/_4$ x 9$^7/_{16}$ x $^3/_8$ in. (400 x 240 x 9.5 mm) (sides)
- 31$^1/_8$ x 9$^1/_4$ x $^3/_8$ in. (790 x 234 x 9.5 mm) (middle shelf)
- 2 pieces 9$^1/_4$ x 7$^5/_8$ x $^3/_8$ in. (234 x 194.5 x 9.5 mm) (shelf dividers)
- 31$^1/_8$ x 15$^3/_8$ x $^1/_4$ in. (791 x 391 x 6 mm) (back)

1

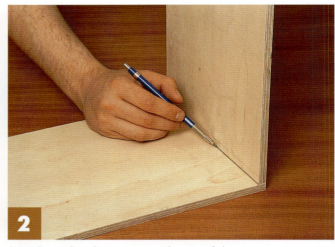

2

The most economical method of cutting a sheet of plywood to the cutting list is to cut the top, sides, and the middle shelf all running across the board, with the shelf dividers then taken from the waste. Mark and cut each component one by one. Before cutting, use a sharp knife to score the face of the board with two parallel lines the width of the kerf. Clamp a straight length of lumber securely to the board as a guide fence for the saw, as shown.

Sort the sides, bottoms, and tops of the unit into groups. On the inside faces of each piece, mark the shoulders of the finger joints using the adjacent component as a guide. Repeat this process for all the joints.

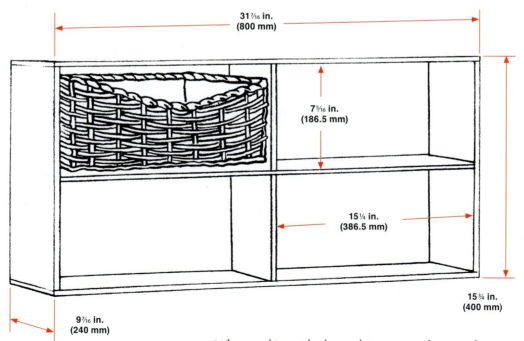

31 7⁄16 in.
(800 mm)

7 5⁄16 in.
(186.5 mm)

15 1⁄4 in.
(386.5 mm)

15 3⁄4 in.
(400 mm)

9 7⁄16 in.
(240 mm)

When working with plywood, it is essential to guard against splitting or breaking out of the surface. Before each cut or router pass, score the top surface with a craft or marking knife.

3

Fit the finger-jointing template in place of the normal dovetail one, inserting a block of MDF to prevent the rear of your work splitting. This block must be square and true on the front edge and should be placed in line with the cut line on the template surface. The smaller piece of MDF in the foreground will keep the template flat.

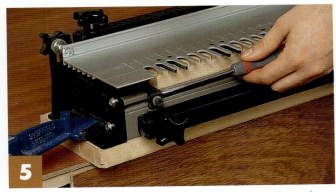

5

The template comes supplied with two ⁵⁄₁₆ in. (8 mm) stop pins. These shift the work over ⁵⁄₁₆ in. (8 mm), thereby allowing the pins and sockets of the finger joints to line up. Insert the stop pins with a screwdriver, then fit and cut the side panels as for the top and bottom.

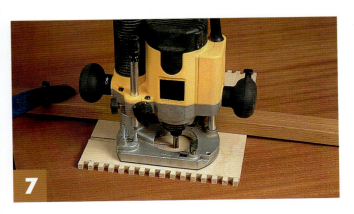

7

4 Clamp the template to the bench with a slight overhang at the front. Fit the ⁷⁄₁₆ in. (11 mm) guide plate (supplied with the template) and a ⁵⁄₁₆ in. (8 mm) straight cutter to your router. Mount the work, ensuring that the upper surface is perfectly aligned with the top of the anti-breakout block and that the work is clamped securely. Use the fine adjuster on the router to lower the cutter exactly to the pencil line drawn in step 2. Rout out all the top and base parts at both ends, working left to right.

6

Sort the sides, tops, and bottoms into separate sets and plane the front and rear edges clean. Use the ⁵⁄₁₆ in. (8 mm) straight cutter in your router and fit a fence set to cut a rabbet ¼ in. (6 mm) wide on the rear edge, inside face for the back. The rabbet should be ³⁄₁₆ in. (10 mm) deep and must stop just short of the pencil lines marked in step 2. Use a ¼ in. (6 mm) chisel to square the ends of the rabbet to the line.

◄ Ascertain the center of the middle shelf and the top and bottom shelves. Scribe two lines ³⁄₈ in. (9 mm) apart with a knife and, using a fence as shown here, rout out the rabbet to take the vertical shelf dividers. The depth of cut for the top and bottom is ³⁄₁₆ in. (10 mm). For the middle shelf, cut only to ⅛ in. (3 mm) on either side. Clean up the rabbets with a chisel. Assemble flat on the bench, check for fit and square, adjust as required, then glue up. For speedy finishing, the use of a belt sander is recommended. Check the internal measurements for the back, cut ¼ in. (6 mm) plywood to fit, and set in place with molding pins.

Corner Cupboard

This corner cupboard with pierced doors is an exercise in cutting simple joints. It uses what is probably the most basic joint of all, the corner halving, made by cutting halfway through the thickness of the lumber with a backsaw (tenon saw) and then removing the waste with a chisel. The outer surface of the wood is left just a little rough, giving the piece a rustic, cottagey feel.

The beading along the top is called "egg and dart." To fit this type of beading correctly will entail some complicated setting-out, so you may wish to replace this with a plain bead of similar size. The piercing can also be simplified. If you wish the piercing to be symmetrical and have both a left and right hand, use a MDF template as a stencil to transfer the design to your doors and flip the template to get both the left and right hand sides.

Paint the cupboard with a coat of rust emulsion then overpaint with jade, rubbed with fine wire wool to reveal a hint of the underlying color. The brass handles and hinges are complemented by the gold paint on the inner faces of the piercing.

Essential Tools & Materials

Tools
- pencil
- measuring tape
- combination square
- sliding bevel
- screwdriver
- hammer
- mallet
- crosscut saw
- backsaw (tenon saw)
- jigsaw with scroll blade
- electric drill, 1/8 in. (3 mm), 3/16 in. (4 mm) and 5/16 in. (8 mm) wood bits, countersink bit
- 1 in. (25 mm) bevel-edge chisel
- jack plane
- block plane
- workbench with vise
- G-clamps
- table-mounted circular saw (optional)
- belt sander (optional)
- electric planer (optional)

Hardware etc.
- 30 countersink 1 3/16 in. (30 mm) x No. 6 screws
- 16 gauge brass countersink screws 1/2 in. (12 mm) x No. 4
- 3/4 in. (20 mm) veneer or molding pins
- 2 magnetic catches
- 2 pairs laid-on brass hinges
- 2 Gothic-style brass handles
- sandpaper in grits 80 and 100
- PVA wood glue
- can of spray paint for stencil

Wood
- 110 1/4 x 2 x 1 in. (2800 x 50 x 25 mm) pine or similar (S4S)
- 86 5/8 x 7 1/16 x 1 in. (2200 x 180 x 25 mm) rough-sawn pine or similar, including 15 3/4 in. (400 mm) for the 2 side panels at 15 3/4 x 6 1/2 x 11/16 in. (400 x 165 x 18 mm)
- 126 x 4 x 3/8 in. (3200 x 100 x 9 mm) tongue-and-groove pine or similar.
- 19 11/16 x 15 3/4 x 1/2 in. (500 x 400 x 12 mm) MDF or plywood
- 3/4 in. (20 mm) egg and dart molding

1

2

Make two frames from 2 x 1 in. (50 x 25 mm) sections, with the outside dimensions of one frame 11 x 15¾ in. (280 x 400 mm), and 11 ¹³⁄₁₆ x 15¾ in. (300 x 400 mm) for the other. Cut four lengths at 15¾ in. (400 mm), two at 11 in. (280 mm) and two at 11 ¹³⁄₁₆ in. (300 mm), and mark the width of the lumber on the faces at the ends of all lengths and half the width, using a marking gauge. Cut the corner halving joints as shown. Glue up and clamp each frame, ensuring that they are square.

Join the two frames together, using the edge of your bench to ensure that they are square. The wider frame overlaps the other, giving an equal length. Glue and screw using three 1³⁄₁₆ in. (30 mm) screws.

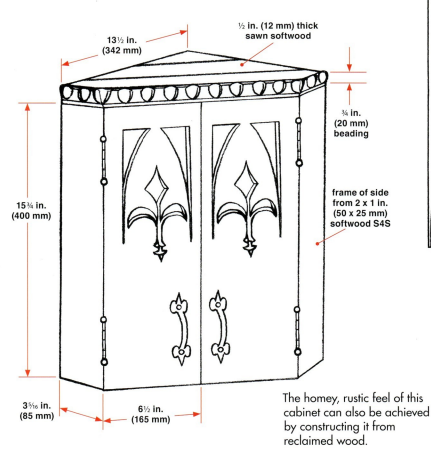

13½ in. (342 mm)

½ in. (12 mm) thick sawn softwood

¾ in. (20 mm) beading

15¾ in. (400 mm)

frame of side from 2 x 1 in. (50 x 25 mm) softwood S4S

3⁵⁄₁₆ in. (85 mm)

6½ in. (165 mm)

The homey, rustic feel of this cabinet can also be achieved by constructing it from reclaimed wood.

This template for the cutout on the doors is shown here at 50% of actual size. Make sure that any variations match the dimensions of the doors.

Prepare the sawn lumber. You need two doors at 15¾ x 6½ x ¹¹⁄₁₆ in. (400 x 165 x 18 mm), two side panels at 15¾ x 3⁵⁄₁₆ x ¾ in. (400 x 85 x 20 mm), one top at 6 ¹¹⁄₁₆ x 13 x ½ in. (170 x 330 x 12 mm), and the other top at 5⅛ x 19⁵⁄₁₆ x ½ in. (130 x 490 x 12 mm). The idea is to keep some of the rough quality of the lumber, but not so much as to give you splinters; a belt sander run along the face is the best method. To plane down the rear face of the lumbers, use an electric plane—don't plane the front faces!

Plane a 45-degree bevel on the inner edges of the side panels; this bevel is attached to the hinges. Measuring from the back of each panel, the bevel needs to be in excess of the thickness of the doors: ¾ in. (22 mm) is a good dimension, and will leave a small flat. The hinge pin sits up to this flat. Screw the sides to the frames, recessing the screws a little. If you wish, you can fill in these screw holes prior to painting the cabinet.

Sit the assembly over the MDF to form the base of the cupboard. Draw around the inside of the frame. When you draw inside the side bevels, take your line up to the small flat at the front of the bevel on each side and join these two points with a straight edge. Check the base for square and ensure both sides are equal because this base will govern the finished shape of the cupboard. Cut out the shape you have drawn and finish off with a plane. Place the side and frame assembly up to the MDF and check the fit. Butt up the doors from the small flat on the side panels, sitting them on the MDF.

TIP

As a way of ensuring that each of the 2 x 1 in. (50 x 25 mm) frames are square before gluing and screwing them together, clamp each frame to the corner of the Workmate.

Reach inside the cupboard and mark the position of each door at the hinge edge. Join the marks with a straightedge. Make sure you are accurate, otherwise the doors will not meet correctly when closed. Cut to the line, plane true, and then screw the frame assembly to the MDF. Line the inside of the frames with the tongue-and-groove lengths; start at one corner and work forward, nailing each length once the entire side has been fitted. The final length on each side will need to be cut along its length to suit.

Take the two parts for the top, the wider being to the rear of the top. Place it on the cupboard and mark the 45-degree angles from the underside. Cut and screw down to the frame. The front part of the top is a little more complicated, since it needs to be cut as a lozenge shape. It butts up to the other part of the top and is flush to the frame at the back, but has an overhang of ¾ in. (20 mm) at the sides and the front. The join of the beading should be at a proper place in the design, allowing the pattern of the beading to continue uninterrupted as the miters are made.

8 Take a length of beading and cut a 67.5 degree miter with the front of the cut in the center of one of the darts. Hold this length up to the front of the top and choose another dart center at the far end. Cut back at 67.5 degrees from this new point. The short points at the rear of the beading will determine the length of the front of the top, hence the overhang, which you should duplicate for the overhang of the sides.

Fit the beading to the top with molding pins, leaving an upstand to form a false cornice. Fit the hinges to the sides at regular spacing, try the doors in place, and adjust as required by planing. There should be a gap all around the doors of about ⅟₃₂ in. (1 mm).

When the doors fit, cut a template from some MDF. Cut out the template with a jigsaw, ensuring the edges are square and smooth. Place the template over the door and spray on some paint, making sure that you get into all the corners. Flip the template and spray the other door. Cut both doors with a jigsaw. Sand off excess paint. Hang the doors, fit the handles and catches. Fill all screw holes with filler, and paint.

Adirondack Chair

This style of sturdy and extremely comfortable patio chair is common throughout North America, where it is called an Adirondack chair, the name deriving from the range of mountains in upper New York State. All the lumbers are simply screwed and glued together, using no joints. Start by making the footstool, and when you have gained confidence, tackle the chair.

It is possible to construct this chair from almost any lumber, even 11/16 in. (18 mm) exterior-grade or marine plywood. If cost is of little concern, teak or iroko would be superb. I used secondhand mahogany; it was poor quality, had been stored in inadequate conditions, and was designated as flooring grade, but it was ludicrously cheap and basically sound.

If you feel that the sloping back of the chair is beyond your capabilities, make the chair with a 90-degree back and straight slats screwed to the back of the final seating slat, which would be straight, as opposed to the curved one shown here. To finish, I used a two-part epoxy coating. This is expensive and tricky to apply, but once wood is properly coated with epoxy, it becomes totally stable and virtually maintenance-free. Stains, polyurethane varnish and gloss paint are acceptable for the finish, but you will have to revarnish or paint your chair every four or five summers.

Essential Tools & Materials

Tools
- pencil
- straightedge
- measuring tape
- square
- marking gauge
- sliding bevel
- string
- screwdriver
- backsaw (tenon saw)
- panel saw
- jigsaw
- power drill, 1/8 in. (3 mm), 3/16 in. (4 mm), 1/4 in. (6 mm), and 5/16 in. (8 mm) wood bits, size 8 plug cutter
- block plane
- jack plane
- workbench
- belt sander (optional)
- orbital (palm) sander (optional)
- beam compass (optional)
- spokeshave (optional)

Hardware etc.
- 200 zinc-plated countersink screws 1½ in. (38 mm) x No. 8
- 40 zinc-plated countersink screws 1¾ in. (45 mm) x No. 8
- 4 brass bolts 2½ x ¼ in. (65 x 6 mm) with nuts and washers
- epoxy wood glue (system 106 or equivalent)
- sandpaper in grits 80 to 300

Wood
- 8 pieces 23⅝ x 2 x 1 in. (600 x 50 x 25 mm) (seat slats)
- 2 pieces 35⁷⁄₁₆ x 5 ¹⁵⁄₁₆ x 1 in. (900 x 150 x 25 mm) (side rails)
- 2 pieces 19 ¹¹⁄₁₆ x 4 x 1 in. (500 x 100 x 25 mm) (legs)
- 2 pieces 7⅞ x 4 x 1 in. (200 x 100 x 25 mm) (armrest brackets)
- 2 pieces 29½ x 7⅞ x 1 in. (750 x 200 x 25 mm) (armrests)
- 27½ x 6 ¹¹⁄₁₆ x 1 in. (700 x 170 x 25 mm) (curved seat slat/back joining rib)
- 2 pieces 23⅝ x 3⁹⁄₁₆ x 1 in. (600 x 90 x 25 mm) (back braces)
- 2 pieces 24⅜ x 4 x 1 in. (620 x 100 x 25 mm) (outer back slats)
- 2 pieces 28¾ x 4 x 1 in. (730 x 100 x 25 mm) (inner back slats)
- 33⁷⁄₁₆ x 5⅛ x 1 in. (850 x 130 x 25 mm) (center back slat)
- 27½ x 2 x 2 in. (700 x 50 x 50 mm) (strengthening blocks)

Footstool

1

◀ The upper and lower radii of the stool rails are 29½ in. (750 mm), with the centers taken from two different positions. Set this out on some scrap plywood or paper first. Draw a line 22⁷⁄₁₆ in. (570 mm) long, divide it in half, and draw a line 2³⁄₁₆ in. (55 mm) at right angles to the center. Extend the line back along the 2³⁄₁₆ in. (55 mm) until it is 29½ in. (750 mm) in total. This is the position of your first center. Set your beam compass or string and pencil accordingly and strike the upper arc. Where the arc touches the 22⁷⁄₁₆ in. (570 mm) line, square off 1½ in. (38 mm) at one end and 2¹⁵⁄₁₆ in. (75 mm) at the other. These two new lines give you the position of the second center by simply scribing an arc at 29½ in. (750 mm) from the end of each line; where the arcs intersect is the second center point. Cut out the shape with a jigsaw and use it as a template for the other rail. Do not cut to the 1½ in. (38 mm) line, but leave the rail overlong at this stage. Lay each rail over the leg section, clamp them together, and rest on a flat surface. Mark the baseline of the rail by scribing from the table, cut, and check. Mark and cut any overhang at the wider end of the rail, which needs to finish flush with the back edge of the vertical leg.

2

When you are happy that the assembly sits flat on the surface, drill and bolt the two parts together, but do not over-tighten. Next, cut out all the slats, rounding the first slat if you wish. When they are all cut to length and arrised, lay them out together and mark out for the screw holes. Come in half the width of a rail from the end of each slat, and mark two equidistant screw holes for each end of each slat. With an ⁵⁄₁₆ in. (8 mm) bit, drill down about ³⁄₁₆ in. (10 mm) for the plugs, then drill through with a ³⁄₁₆ in. (4 mm) bit for the screw shank.

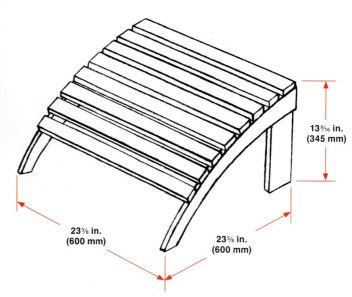

13⁵⁄₁₆ in. (345 mm)

23⅝ in. (600 mm)

23⅝ in. (600 mm)

An alternative design for these chairs and stools is to use mortise and tenon joints; the method here is just as sturdy—and easier!

3 Attach all of the slats in place one by one, ⁹⁄₁₆ in. (15 mm) apart, using two MDF or plywood spacers, drilling through the screw shank hole into the rails with a ⅛ in. (3 mm) pilot hole. Attach one slat at a time and check that the two rails remain parallel and that you are fixing the slats square to the rails. Do not drive the screws fully home or glue up.

4 From scrap pieces matching the footstool, cut a sufficient number of plugs to fill the screw holes, using a guide for the plug cutter clamped to the wood. The guide can be made from ¼ in. (6 mm) MDF or plywood. When you have enough plugs, disassemble the stool and position the screws, nuts, and bolts and keep at hand. Ensure that the work area is dust-free and prepare to glue up (refer to step 15 for details). Before driving in the screws during final assembly, rub each screw thread against a wax candle or some beeswax to drive them home with far less effort.

Chair

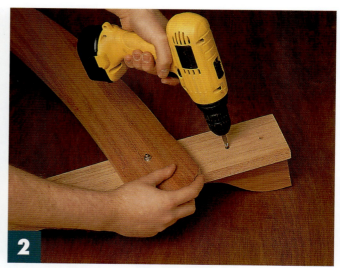

Draw out the rails freehand onto the 35⁷⁄₁₆ x 5 ¹⁵⁄₁₆ in. (900 x 150 mm) lengths. Use the full length, and make sure that the rails are not less than 4 in. (100 mm) wide at any point. The height at the front of the chair rail should match the height of the back of the footstool (about 11 ¹³⁄₁₆ in. [300 mm]). As you have already done for the stool, scribe the back to the bench top while the leg is clamped in position, but this time, instead of cutting the front end of the rail flush to the leg, let it project forward about 4 in. (100 mm) and round it off. Mark the position of the leg on the rail and unclamp. Mark two flats on the front that you have drawn; these will take the front two rails, the uppermost needing to be ⁹⁄₁₆ in. (15 mm) forward of the front of the leg. Draw the flat 2 in. (50 mm), add another ⁹⁄₁₆ in. (15 mm) gap, and then draw the second 2 in. (50 mm) flat. Cut this out with a jigsaw and copy the shape to its pair. Finish off to a smooth surface with a belt sander and bolt the legs to the rails.

The top of the legs will now need to be marked and drilled for the armrest brackets. Remember to drill for the plugs first, then the shank. Drill the pilot holes when you assemble. The brackets can be a simple triangle or a little more ornate; you will get both brackets from one short length. Assemble the seat slats.

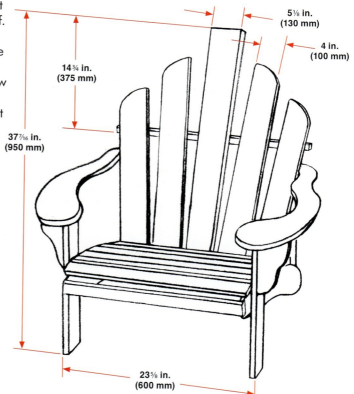

5⅛ in. (130 mm)

4 in. (100 mm)

14¾ in. (375 mm)

37⁷⁄₁₆ in. (950 mm)

23⅝ in. (600 mm)

3

When marking out the curvature of the final seat slat, the most effective method is to use a steel ruler as shown. As you increase the pressure at either end of the ruler, you can alter the ellipse of the curve: equal pressure gives an equal curve. The lumber you use should be wide enough to leave a waste piece of about 2 in. (50 mm) at its narrowest point; this will form the reinforcing rib behind the back. When you have decided on the amount of curvature you want for the back slats, mark and cut with a jigsaw.

4

Drill the holes for screwing the final slat to the rails and mark the centerline. Now position a flat across the curve 2 in. (50 mm) each side of the centerline, then use the slat spacer to mark a gap of 9/16 in. (15 mm) and after that a further 4 in. (100 mm) flat, as shown. When making the chair, use the actual back slats as a guide from which to mark off, prior to shaping them, rather than separate guide ones. Plane to the lines of the flats and then clamp them in place on the seat assembly, checking slats and rails for square.

5

TIP

When using countersink screws, make the counterbore into the lumber about 3/16 in. (10 mm) deep; any less, and you will find it difficult to cut the plugs accurately.

◀ Position the waste piece left over from step 7 by using the spacers, 9/16 in. (15 mm) away from the clamped slat. Use a small waste piece about 1 in. (25 mm) thick to transfer the flats to form the front profile of the reinforcing rail for the back slats. Cut to the scribed lines with a jigsaw.

6

Unclamp the final slat from the assembly and screw five strengthening blocks, each about 3⁹⁄₁₆ in. (90 mm) long, to the underside, to give an added glue area to the base of the back slats. Any strong hardwood will do for the strengthening blocks. Screw the blocks from underneath to the rear of the final rail, running along each flat. Plane them flush using a block or a jack plane to achieve a consistent bevel of about 85 degrees.

7 Place the final slat edge down on the workbench and lay out the five pre-cut slats that form the back. The two 24⅜ in. (620 mm) long back slats are placed at the outside, then the 28¾ in. (730 mm) slats, with the longest at 33⁷⁄₁₆ in. (850 mm), placed in the middle. Try to get an even distance between each slat at the top. Position the waste piece from step 3 about two-thirds of the way along the back to form a rib. This takes trial and error; you may find you have to reduce or increase the splay of the back, or lengthen the flats on the rib. When the fit is acceptable, mark the back slats where the rib sits and set aside. Mark each slat for the top profile and the bottom angle. Cut to fit with a jigsaw.

8

When cut, drill and screw together and place the assembly back on the rails. At this stage the back is fragile and will flop about, so take care. Check the fit of the rib again and, if good, drill through the back slats, two holes per slat, taking great care that the drill does not burst through the face of the rib. Screw the rib and back slat temporarily in place to provide some rigidity—every other screw hole will be sufficient at this stage. From the narrowest point of the rib draw a smooth line that follows the curvature of the back to each end. Draw a half-round to finish level with the two end back slats. Remove, cut the waste with a jigsaw, sand or plane smooth, and refit.

Fit the two braces that support the back underneath the back rib. Bolt them to the inside of the back of the rails. Leave the bottom width of the braces at 3⁹⁄₁₆ in. (90 mm) and taper the upper end so that it is the same width as the rib. Cut the bottom as a half-round and the top as a compound miter, meeting the back face of the outer back slat and the underside of the rib (see right photo for detail). Mark the compound miter by scribing from the relevant faces, and use a sharp block plane to plane down to the lines (left photo). When correctly shaped, drill and screw the top in place and use a bolt to attach the brace to the bottom to the rail.

The key factors influencing the shape of the arms are: at the front, you need enough space for a large gin and tonic, and the back needs to curl around the outside of the outer edge of the outer back slat and butt up to the outer face of the braces. The best way to achieve this is to use a scrap piece of MDF or plywood and obtain the shape by a process of trial and error. Use a level to position the arms, then mark the underside where it meets the brace. Fit a small block at this mark and then screw the arm down onto the block. The front of the arm is screwed down into the front leg and armrest bracket. When gluing up, pour a little glue into these holes as you are screwing into end grain.

TIP

When gluing up, cover your workbench with newspaper to catch any drips of adhesive.

11 When applying epoxy resin, use rubber gloves, mix accurately according to the manufacturer's instructions, and work quickly—drips and spillage can be cleaned off later. Mix only as much glue as you can use in 25 minutes. Glue the legs, rails, and slats together, screwing and bolting as you go, then mix more for the plugs. Let everything cure for a day, then clean off any excess glue with a chisel and sandpaper and cut the plugs flush.

Birdhouse

This project is designed to be constructed with the minimum of tools and skills, although you can of course develop the basic idea. You will need to be aware of two things: first, the type of birds you wish to attract. The dimensions here are for the smaller songbirds; larger or more unusual birds will require different dimensions.

Second, you must make entry to the birdhouse by predators impossible. The chimney and bargeboards on the roof increase the weight, making it harder for the predator to dislodge, the extreme angle of the roof allows no footholds, and the epoxy glue coating around the entrance hole makes it difficult to enlarge the entrance hole by chewing to gain entrance.

Looking down the list of tools required, there is one tool that is a little specialized. A gouge is a curved chisel, mainly used in the workshop for fitting curved moldings to a miter. Here I used it to achieve a "Hansel-and-Gretel" look on the roof tiles, but you could just as easily use a normal chisel and have rectangular roof tiles.

Paint your birdhouse with ordinary emulsion, using a crackle glaze applied between two complementary shades, and finish with two coats of exterior varnish.

Essential Tools & Materials

Tools
- pencil
- measuring tape
- square
- sliding bevel
- knife
- jigsaw with scrolling blade and straight cutting blade
- power drill, ¼ and 1 in. (6 and 25 mm) wood bits
- ¾ in. (19 mm) gouge
- jack plane
- block plane
- workbench
- G-clamp

Hardware etc.
- sandpaper grit 100
- two-part epoxy glue

Wood
- 2 pieces 8⅝ x 4¾ in. x ½ in. (220 x 120 x 12 mm) exterior-grade plywood (front and back)
- 2 pieces 4 x 4⁵⁄₁₆ x ½ in. (100 x 110 x 12 mm) exterior-grade plywood (sides)
- 4 x 3 ¹³⁄₁₆ x ½ in. (100 x 97 x 12 mm) exterior-grade plywood (base)
- 2 pieces 6¼ x 6¼ x ½ in. (160 x 160 x 12 mm) exterior-grade plywood (roof)
- 7⅞ x 5 ¹⁵⁄₁₆ x ¼ in. (200 x 150 x 6 mm) exterior-grade plywood
- small hardwood waste piece
- 2 x ¼ in. (6 mm) dowel pegs
- 17¾ x 15 x ½ in. (450 x 380 x 12 mm) exterior-grade plywood
- 7⅞ x 5 ¹⁵⁄₁₆ x ¼ in. (200 x 150 x 6 mm) exterior-grade plywood

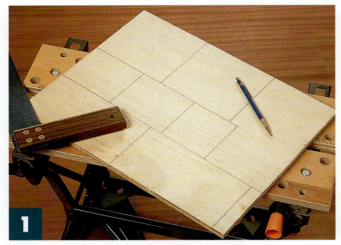

1 Referring to the diagram and cutting list, mark out a piece of ½ in. (12 mm) exterior-grade plywood. In the photograph the thicker lines are the saw cuts, otherwise known as the kerf.

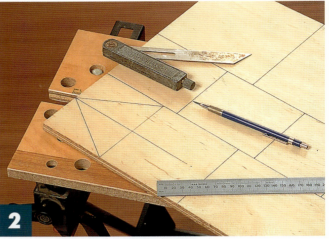

2 To achieve the pitch of the roof, first mark a centerline through the front and back panels. Measure up from the baseline of the front 4⁵⁄₁₆ in. (110 mm) to give the height of the side panels. Join the top of the centerline to the end of the 4⁵⁄₁₆ in. (110 mm) line; this gives the angle of the roof pitch. Set a sliding bevel to this angle and mark the angle on the back. Cut out all the parts with a jigsaw or handsaw.

3 Place one of the sides of the roof in your vise or workbench and plane the angle of the ridge across the grain, using your sliding bevel to check that the angle is true. Repeat for the matching piece.

As a further defense against predators, you can screw the lid of the birdhouse to the walls.

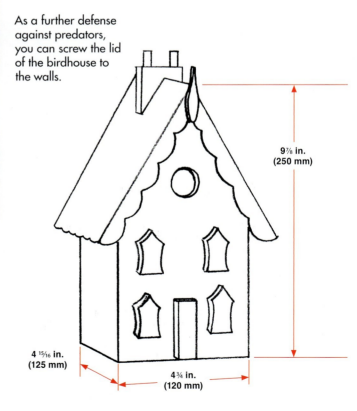

9⅞ in. (250 mm)

4¹⁵⁄₁₆ in. (125 mm)

4¾ in. (120 mm)

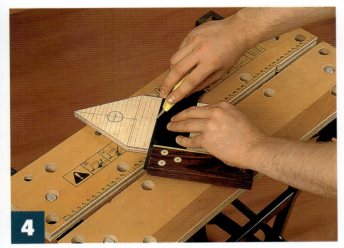

Mark a line across the faces every ⁵⁄₁₆ in. (8 mm) or so; accuracy is not of paramount importance, but try to keep the lines square and parallel. Cut along each line with a craft knife held at an angle. Move along about a millimeter or so and make another cut with the knife at the opposite angle to create a V-shaped groove. When all the lines are cut, brush out the waste. Mark the entrance hole to 1 in. (25 mm) for small birds and 1⅛ in. (28 mm) for slightly larger birds.

Mark out the roof tiles as shown. The lines are 1 in. (25 mm) apart, the width of a standard ruler, and the tiles are the width of the gouge. Each run is offset from its predecessor to resemble real roofing tiles. Cut the final line of tiles to its profile, using a jigsaw fitted with a scrolling blade. Drill the entrance hole using a flat bit or a hole saw. Measure and cut the chimney stack from some scrap wood. Use the sliding bevel to determine the angle of the cutout, and drill two ¼ in. (6 mm) holes in the top for the dowels.

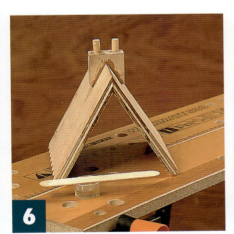

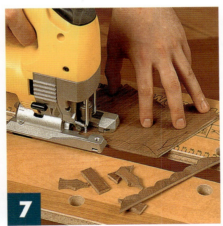

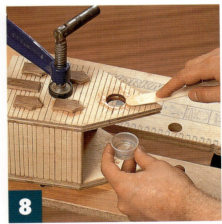

Position the chimneystack so that it acts as a simple clamp to hold the roof members together when you glue them up.

Cut the fake door, windows, finial, and bargeboards from the small scrap piece of ¼ in. (6 mm) plywood, using a jigsaw. Use some stylistic freedom here!

Glue up the house, using one clamp to hold the box. Liberally smear a layer of glue around the entrance hole to strengthen it against predators. Attach the bargeboards and finial to the roof assembly.

Mailbox

This project introduces cold-form bending, a technique that can, in relatively small projects, replace specialized steam bending; even better, unlike steam bending, it requires no expensive equipment. It also uses the fillet joint—a bead of viscous epoxy glue smeared across two adjacent surfaces, with the bead providing the actual joint. It is stronger than the lumber it joins and has no loss of strength when used as a gap-filling compound up to ¼ in. (6 mm) wide. Here, it is used to join the roof to the carcass.

To construct the roof, use layers of thin plywood or veneers built up to a thickness of 5⁄16 in. (8 mm). Use paper-backed veneers, which are cheap and don't tear or split along the grain. Since only small amounts are needed for this project, see if local cabinetmakers or joinery shops have some scrap pieces.

The mailbox here was fully veneered with maple, but you can stain or paint the carcass and use aero or skin plywood for the roof. This is a flexible plywood thinner than 1⁄16 in. (2 mm) that will bend to a radius of less than 4 in. (100 mm).

The finish is two-pack polyurethane matte varnish, with the inside painted with bright red eggshell.

Essential Tools & Materials

Tools
- pencil
- measuring tape
- square
- sliding bevel
- Flexicurve or French curves
- craft knife or scalpel
- jigsaw
- power drill, 1⁄16 in. (2 mm), 3⁄16 in. (4 mm), and ¼ in. (6 mm) wood bits
- belt sander
- ½ in. (12 mm) and 1 in. (25 mm) bevel-edge chisels
- jack plane
- block plane
- workbench with vise
- G-clamps

Hardware etc.
- 5⅛ in. (130 mm) brass or stainless steel piano hinge and screws
- small brass cabinet lock and screws
- sandpaper grades 100 to 240
- PVA wood glue
- two-part epoxy glue and colloidal silica

Wood
- 25⁹⁄16 x 17⅛ x ⅜ in. (650 x 435 x 9 mm) exterior-grade plywood
- 25⁹⁄16 x 17⅛ in. (650 x 435 mm) sheet of paper-backed veneer (optional)
- 25⁹⁄16 x 25⁹⁄16 (650 x 650 mm) sheet of paper-backed veneer or aero/skin plywood
- 39⅝ x 2 15⁄16 x 2 in. (1000 x 75 x 50 mm) sawn pine or similar

1 Cut three 13 in. (330 mm) lengths of 2 15/16 x 2 in. (75 x 50 mm) lumber, plane or belt-sand the faces smooth, and select one block as a pattern. Mark the centerline and two square lines 11 13/16 in. (300 mm) apart, and use a Flexicurve or French curves to draw a slow curve with a slight upstand at the ends. The curve should lie roughly in the center of the block. Cut to the line with a jigsaw. If the blade wanders during cutting, correct this with a belt sander. Use the pattern to replicate the marks on the other two blocks.

2 Glue each set of three formers together with PVA, then clamp and let dry. Cut the 3/8 in. (9 mm) plywood to the sizes proscribed while the blocks are drying. Plane a bevel on the two short sides of the base, making the angle the same as the sides. Fit each half of the completed block in the vise and use a belt sander to obtain a good fit of the two parts. Ensure that the two surfaces not only fit but that they are as near as possible square to the edges.

3

Cut the skin plywood or veneer into eight sheets of 6¼ x 12½ in. (160 x 320 mm), four sheets running with the grain and four against. Place a sheet of newspaper over the concave section of the block and lay each sheet of veneer in place, alternating the grain direction. Lay another sheet of newspaper over the final sheet, place the convex block in place, and apply hand pressure. Check that each sheet of veneer is tightly compressed up against its neighbor and that you have an equal amount of overhang at each end. Unpack the stack and lay aside in reverse order. Mix the epoxy glue—with a 5:1 ratio you will need about ⅔ oz. (20 mL) of resin and ⅛ oz. (4 mL) of fast hardener. Wear gloves, work quickly, and insert both sheets of newspaper. Clamp and clean off any excess glue.

4 When dry—normally about two hours at 68°F (20°C)—unclamp and remove the newspaper and excess glue using a belt sander fitted with 120 grit or higher sandpaper. You can accelerate the drying time by gently applying heat via a heat gun or a blow dryer. Use a block plane to get the edges exactly flush, starting with the front edge, and then using a square to mark the two ends. Plane toward the center to avoid splitting the ends. Lay the edge of the roof section over the front and back walls and check the fit—1/64 in. (0.5 mm) either way is acceptable. Sand or plane the roofline to achieve the fit.

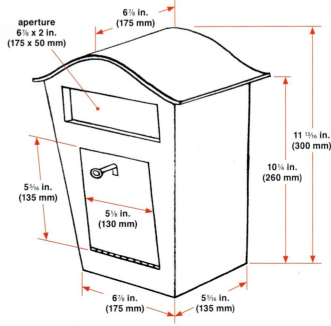

aperture
6⅞ x 2 in.
(175 x 50 mm)

6⅞ in. (175 mm)

11 13/16 in. (300 mm)

10¼ in. (260 mm)

5 5/16 in. (135 mm)

5⅛ in. (130 mm)

6⅞ in. (175 mm)

5 5/16 in. (135 mm)

5 Mark out the front panel to the given measurements, drill a hole in the waste parts, and remove the waste with a jigsaw. Cut as close as you can with the blade and clean up with a chisel. (If you have a router, use it for this job and cut the corners of the openings square.) Test the replacement door panel for fit: you should have a gap of less than ¹⁄₆₄ in. (0.5 mm) all around, except for the bottom edge, which needs a gap of ³⁄₁₆ in. (4 mm) to accommodate the hinge.

6 Cut the veneers, if you intend to use them. Each component will need to be cut with about a ³⁄₈ in. (10 mm) overhang all around. If you are using paper-backed veneers for convenience, sharp scissors are the best method of cutting them. When you come to the apertures, use a sharp craft knife or a scalpel to exactly mark each corner with two right-angled cuts. Turn the veneer face up and join the marks using a steel ruler, taking care not to cut past the pre-cut corners.

7 Apply glue to the veneers and clamp up; protect the veneer with paper, and don't clamp too tightly. When dry, clean up and cut the edges of the veneer flush as follows: front, back and door, all edges; sides, the top and bottom only; leave all the overhangs on the base.

8

Cut the piano hinge to the same size as the bottom of the door and screw in place. The center of the knuckle should be exactly over the inner edge of the door. Screw to the front panel and plane the door if necessary.

9

Unscrew the door and remove the waste for the lock. Fit the lock and striking plate, mark for the keyhole, and cut with drills and chisel. Do not refit the door. To increase the viscosity of the glue mix and prevent it from running down the joins, add up to 35% colloidal silica. When dry, shave off the overhanging veneers from the box with a block plane. Make another mix as before and glue the roof in place upside down. Pour in a generous amount of glue and use a rounded spatula to form the ¼ in. (6 mm) fillet joint when the glue has started to cure. Replace the door and sand the box smooth.

Templates

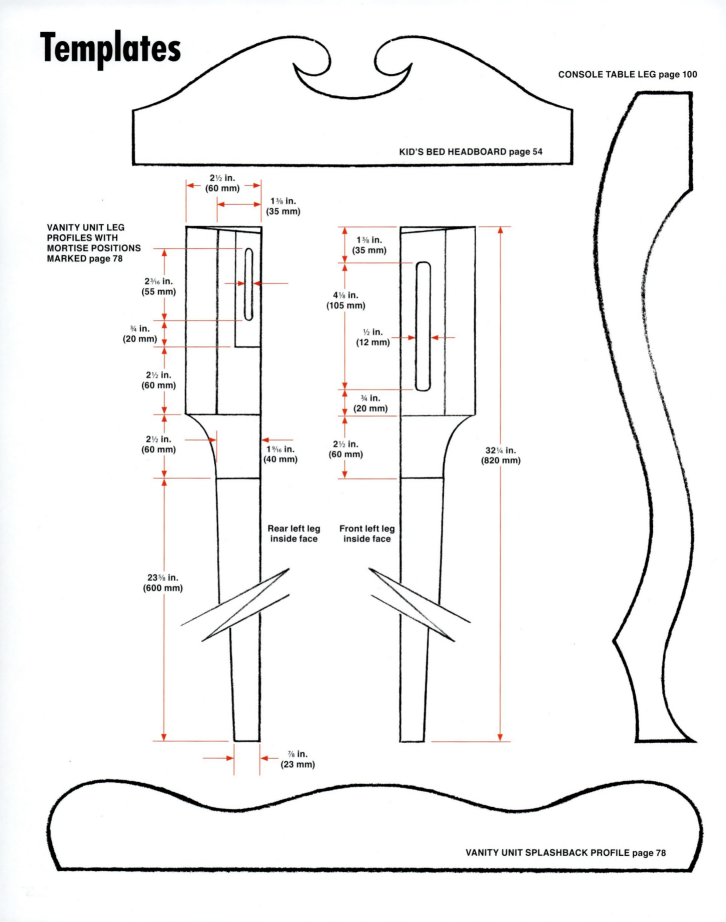

CONSOLE TABLE LEG page 100

KID'S BED HEADBOARD page 54

2½ in.
(60 mm)

1⅜ in.
(35 mm)

**VANITY UNIT LEG
PROFILES WITH
MORTISE POSITIONS
MARKED page 78**

2³⁄₁₆ in.
(55 mm)

¾ in.
(20 mm)

2½ in.
(60 mm)

2½ in.
(60 mm)

1⁹⁄₁₆ in.
(40 mm)

23⅝ in.
(600 mm)

1⅜ in.
(35 mm)

4⅛ in.
(105 mm)

½ in.
(12 mm)

¾ in.
(20 mm)

2½ in.
(60 mm)

32¼ in.
(820 mm)

Rear left leg
inside face

Front left leg
inside face

⅞ in.
(23 mm)

VANITY UNIT SPLASHBACK PROFILE page 78

Index